Lord Of The
Abandoned

Lord Of The Abandoned

Ray Saunders

Chosen Books

A Division of Baker Book House Co
Grand Rapids, Michigan 49516

Library of Congress Cataloging-in-Publication Data

Saunders, Ray, 1936–
    Lord of the abandoned / Ray Saunders.
        p.   cm.
    ISBN 0-8007-9188-6
    1. Church work with women—Brazil.   2. Church work with children—
Brazil.   3. Saunders, Ray, 1936–   .   I. Title.
BV4445.S28   1991
253'.0981—dc20   91-19367
                                                                                CIP

Dedicated to:

The Lord Jesus Christ

As we have heard, so have we seen.
Psalm 48:8

Acknowledgments

I am deeply indebted to the following people for their part in the production of this book:

My wife, Heather   for the inestimable contribution she has made in the relating of this family story. Without her encouragement, cooperation and patience it would not have been possible.

Anne Severance   for her skill and discernment in the editing of the original manuscript.

Jane Campbell and Ann McMath   for their professional encouragement to complete the project.

Graham Ash, Sue Harris, Len LeSourd and Eric Wood   for their practical and helpful appraisal of the manuscript.

John W. Beach   for his introduction to Chosen Books.

Our prayer partners   who prayed this book into being and who continue to pray that God will use it to bring others to a personal knowledge of "The Lord of the Abandoned."

Contents

Who can be compared with God enthroned
on high? Far below him are the heavens
and the earth; he stoops to look, and
lifts the poor from the dirt,
and the hungry from the garbage dump,
and sets them among princes!

Psalm 113:5–8, LB

1
Twenty Meters from Death

For you have delivered my soul
from death and my feet from
stumbling, that I may walk before
God in the light of life.

Psalm 56:13

I once prayed a dangerous prayer: "Lord, I want to know Your reality. If You will show me Your living presence, I'll stop pretending and start all over with You, *whatever it takes*. . . ."

This was no trivial prayer from a grown man. As a Christian for 24 years, an active churchman and a respectable family man, I had been so busy about the Lord's business that I had failed to get to know Him personally. From the day I sent out that cry from the heart as a challenge to the living God, dramatic things began to happen. I will never forget one answer to my prayer nearly three years later.

My memories of that cloudless January afternoon of 1976 in Brazil are razor-sharp. I recall standing with Sue and Andrew, our teenage daughter and son, on the silver sands of the tropical beach of Suarao, south of Santos. Looking up into a benign blue sky, I praised God for our family's safe arrival after a hazardous journey through the mountains of the Serra. This mountain range forms a steep escarpment running down to the sea. Maneuvering a vehicle along the narrow road beside precipitous cliffs requires tremendous concentration and skill and provides a hair-raising ride for the traveler. With a profound sense of relief, we had successfully negotiated the hairpin twists and turns and were now settling into a friend's beach house, anticipating a brief vacation from our mission assignment of administering a student hostel in the city of Sao Paulo.

Scanning the wide expanse of near-deserted coastline while Sue and Andrew went racing down the beach, I allowed myself a moment to revel in the burning rays of the sun as muscles and nerves responded to its warmth. I drank in the peace and beauty after our tiring journey, indulging in the luxury of soft sand trickling through my toes and smiling at the foamy-white crests of the waves as they chased each other across the surface of the sea.

Back at the house my wife, Heather, was unpacking the suitcases and caring for our four-year-old son, Timothy. The two of them planned to join us later for a swim. Meanwhile, not heeding the strong warning left by our host that this stretch of beach was dangerous for unsupervised swimmers, I stepped into the water to test its depth and the swiftness of the current.

"Lord, what a perfect setting for our first holiday in Brazil!" I whispered, lulled by the balmy ocean breeze. "You are such a wonderful, loving God to us."

Wading out a few meters, I gazed back at the shoreline. Events since my dangerous prayer in August 1973 flashed through my mind in quick succession—the subsequent encounter with the Lord, Heather's illness and miraculous healing, our call to Brazil and our year spent working in the mission hostel.

Preoccupied with this reminiscence, I stepped into an unexpected deep hole in the sea bed. Losing my footing, I was thrown into the water, face down. I began to swim, instinctively, but as I flailed about, trying desperately to reach the shore, wave after wave crashed over my head and a great tidal undertow tugged me farther out to sea.

In those moments it was as if I were surrounded by hideous monsters, leering at me, mocking me and jeering, "Now you are in our power! We have you and there is no escape!" I remember seeing in my mind a vision of the sea goddess who is worshiped by thousands of spiritists along the four-and-a-half-thousand-mile coastline of Brazil. Little boats containing her image are decorated with flowers and gifts and pushed out to sea as offerings of appeasement. Ironically this was her festival season. The darkness, fear and panic that engulfed me were ample proof of the reality of hell and of demons.

Then, just as suddenly, came another voice, as real as all the evil ones crowding my consciousness. This voice, however, was very different. Clear as a bell, I heard, *Turn over and float on your back.*

I obeyed instantly, and peace flooded my soul. For the first time since entering the water, I now felt the undeniable presence of the Lord with me. Surely it was His voice I had heard. The fantastic truth dawned that I was in God's hands, and no demon or devil or sea goddess could snatch me away!

A great wave of gratitude swelled in my heart and there, floating on my back in the water, I held a private festival of praise to God. I thanked Him for His gift of salvation and for His presence in those dangerous waters. I praised Him for who He is—the Creator and controller of the universe and all its elements. The words of Psalm 23 came vividly to mind: "You prepare a table before me in the presence of my enemies."

For an indefinite period of time I felt the Lord's nearness, both intimate and awesome. It was as if, like Jesus and one of His early disciples, we were fellowshiping together in a boat on the Sea of Galilee. Buoyed by the joy of being with Him, I knew no fatigue until I became aware gradually that my arms and legs were growing as heavy as lead weights. I could feel them sinking lower and lower into the water. Finally my head went under, and I began to gulp down great mouthfuls of sea water.

Believing that death was near and expecting to be lifted straight into heaven, I prayed quietly, "Lord, into Your hands I commit my spirit."

But the waters parted above me and, to my great surprise, I found myself looking up at blue sky again.

Then I heard that same crystal-clear voice speaking from somewhere behind me. *Throw your head back into the water.*

Again my obedience was instantaneous. Eager to see the One who had spoken to me, I relaxed and followed His instructions. Instead of coming face to face with Jesus, however, I slipped into unconsciousness and remember no more except the final view of water and sky meeting on the horizon behind my head. . . .

Meanwhile the scene on that beach was no longer peaceful. Heather and the children had been dashing frantically along the shore, looking out into the waves for me. Finally they spotted my body being tossed mercilessly to and fro by the sea. Within minutes Heather and Andrew had retrieved my limp form from the heaving seas as Sue looked on in frozen disbelief. My face was waxen, drained of all color, eyes open and fixed, devoid of any spark of life.

As she recounted it later, Heather read the unmistakable signs with a dawning despair. She had seen eyes like that while working for an undertaker in Southampton, England, before our marriage.

What is happening, Lord? she questioned in agonized silence. *Only yesterday You gave Ray a new suit. Surely You didn't provide it for him to wear to his own funeral! And just last night You gave me a verse from Your Word: "Thanks be to God who gives us the victory." Where's the victory in this situation? Death doesn't seem much like victory to me! I can't wish Ray back if You want to keep him with You, as he looks so full of peace. But what about the children and me? You are going to have to give us the victory in this situation. And please, Lord, don't take me from Brazil until the work You called us to do here is finished.*

Heather was brought back to the crisis at hand by Sue's voice calling for help. Released from the icy fear that had paralyzed her upon seeing my lifeless form, Sue now shouted, first in English. Then, realizing she would not be understood, changed her cry to the Portuguese *"Socorro! Socorro!"*

Suddenly, as if from nowhere, dark-skinned, semi-clad figures appeared on all sides. One of them, a husky fellow, said he was a doctor. By the time he arrived, our son Andrew had begun to administer mouth-to-mouth resuscitation. The doctor clapped him on the shoulder and encouraged Andrew to continue while he checked my vital signs. With his hand still on my pulse, the doctor looked up at Heather and shook his head. She spoke the words for him: "My husband is in God's hands."

At that moment my body convulsed and a stream of sea water spewed out of my mouth onto the beach. Then I lay motionless again.

"Quick! Get him to the hospital!" urged Heather. "I believe he's alive!"

A vehicle was rushed across the sand, and I was bundled in to make the short drive to a nearby casualty hospital.

Some time later I became aware of a sharp pain in my back and a terrific thumping on my chest. I could hear many excited voices and the sound of gas escaping from a cylinder.

Someone came up close to my ear and shouted in Portuguese, "What is your name?" She repeated the question slowly and loudly several times.

Out of my extreme exhaustion, I made a mighty effort to reply, knowing I must let someone know I was alive. I tried to answer that my name was Raymond. To my dismay, however, I heard the strangest, most unintelligible sounds coming from my mouth.

How odd. In my mind, everything was so clear. I could hear everything that was being said. I could think and reason normally. And yet I was unable to express coherent sounds or words.

It was as if I were locked in a cocoon or space capsule, able to receive communication from the outside, yet lacking the means of transmitting a message.

Hearing the gibberish I was uttering, the attending physician reported to Heather that I was alive, but was suffering from brain and heart damage.

"There's nothing more we can do for him here," he said. "Since the facilities are better at the main hospital in Santos, we'll transfer him at once."

Heather merely nodded. Quietly, in her heart, she continued her barrage of prayer: *Lord, You've given Ray his life back, but You know he's no use to You as a cabbage! You are able to make him whole. May Your will be done in his life.*

A gust of cool air blew on my face as I was lifted into the ambulance, and I heard Heather's soft voice close by. "The Lord is with you, darling."

With the siren wailing continuously from the roof above my head, the ambulance started down the highway that led to the coffee port of Santos, some thirty kilometers to the north. From the sharp swerves of the emergency vehicle, I could envision other cars pulling over to the side of the road to let us pass. For the second time that afternoon, a great peace filled my being and, within my spirit, there arose silent praises to God.

Suddenly, to my great surprise and delight, my sight came back. When I opened my eyes, I looked into the faces of two nurses who sat opposite me, staring dreamily out of the back window of the ambulance.

One of them glanced down at me and, realizing I was looking back at her, nudged her companion. "Is everything all right?" she asked hesitantly in Portuguese.

I smiled back. "Everything is fine!"

On arrival at the Santa Casa Hospital, I was examined by an

English-speaking doctor, who asked a multitude of questions about my ordeal at sea. He could not understand the report of brain and heart damage as there was no longer any sign of either complication.

"It looks as if you've pulled through," he said with a grin. "We'll soon have you back on your feet. But first you'll need to build up your strength."

Shortly afterward I was comfortably ensconced in a small hospital room, an intravenous saline drip strapped to one arm. I lay there for hours, Heather by my side, reliving the events of the day. I had faced death—first with terrifying foreboding, then with the reality of God's peace and presence. Over and over I asked the question: *Why, Lord? Why did You spare my life when I was more than content to pass into Your glorious, eternal presence?*

During the next few days of rest and recuperation, the Lord answered me through His Word. Scanning the pages of the Bible, my eyes fell on some verses from 2 Samuel 22 that leaped to life:

> "The Lord is my rock, my fortress and my deliverer. . . .
> The waves of death swirled about me; the torrents of destruction overwhelmed me. . . . In my distress I called to the Lord; I called out to my God. From his temple he heard my voice; my cry came to his ears. . . . He reached down from on high and took hold of me; he drew me out of deep waters. He rescued me from my powerful enemy, from my foes, who were too strong for me. They confronted me in the day of my disaster, but the Lord was my support."
> verses 2, 5, 7, 17–19

As I recovered, gaining strength each day, it was easy to pray the words of the Psalms, written by another who had faced death and been delivered on more than one occasion:

> Be at rest once more, O my soul, for the Lord has been good
> to you. For you, O Lord, have delivered my soul from
> death, my eyes from tears, my feet from stumbling, that I
> may walk before the Lord in the land of the living. . . .
> How can I repay the Lord for all his goodness to me? I will
> lift up the cup of salvation and call on the name of the Lord.
> I will fulfill my vows to the Lord in the presence of all his
> people.   Psalm 116:7–9, 12–14

My close new bond with the Lord, initiated that awful day in
the open sea, seemed somehow underlined by a promise in Isaiah:

> But now, this is what the Lord says—he who created you,
> O Jacob, he who formed you, O Israel: "Fear not, for I
> have redeemed you; I have called you by name; you are
> mine. When you pass through the waters, I will be with
> you; and when you pass through the rivers, they will not
> sweep over you. . . . You are precious and honored in my
> sight, and . . . I love you."   Isaiah 43:1, 2, 4

But how had I survived drowning? Or had I actually passed
beyond life for a brief time, only to be resurrected from my
watery grave? I knew that a block of time was missing. The
doctor on the beach had almost despaired of saving me, Heather
had said, and if she had not urged him to call an ambulance. . . .

Whatever His reason for sparing my life, I knew that God had
plans for me, and that the path, while rewarding, would not be
easy. He had posted in His Word a warning as clear as the note
about the hazards of swimming on Suarao Beach:

> For our struggle is not against flesh and blood, but against
> the rulers, against the authorities, against the powers of this

dark world and against the spiritual forces of evil in the heavenly realms. Therefore put on the full armor of God, so that when the day of evil comes, you may be able to stand your ground, and after you have done everything, to stand.

Ephesians 6:12–13

I shared my mounting exhilaration with Heather. God had dramatically laid yet another claim on my life, made it clear that if I was to be abandoned to His will, to be prepared for any challenge ahead, mysterious as it might be, I must learn to listen carefully for His voice, to act decisively when I heard it and to arm myself against future assaults of the enemy.

Now, with the long hours stretching before me like an empty canvas, my mind sketched scenes from the past. . . .

2
In Quest of Real Life

The Spirit and the bride say, "Come!"
And let him who hears say, "Come!"
Whoever is thirsty, let him come;
and whoever wishes, let him take
the free gift of the water of life.

Revelation 22:17

They came, those sights and sounds from my childhood, in staccato bursts of remembered impressions—the hill on which I lived in the busy and vulnerable port of Southampton, England, overlooking the town and the air base; the terrifying whine of buzz bombs; the swoop and spin of planes—feisty Spitfires and dogged Messerschmitts—battling to win the blue skies over England.

Death was soon no stranger to me. As World War II escalated, my dad, a quiet and sensitive man, a policeman by trade, was given the dreary task of notifying the next of kin that a husband or son had been injured, or, most dreaded news of all, that the loved one was missing in action or killed and would not be coming home. Mum worked tirelessly in her garden willing the soil to produce food enough for our family of six, along with a steady stream of boarders who came to work in the factories.

A nightly ritual that quickly ceased to be a lark for my sister, two brothers and myself was carrying our bed linens to a nearby air raid shelter to sleep. I recall leaving our shelter at daybreak on a spring morning in 1941 to find that the roof of our house had been shorn off, leaving us among the growing number of homeless. I will never forget the sight that greeted us. The street next to ours had received a direct hit, flattening all the houses on both sides and leaving a gaping crater in the middle. Later reports named neighbors who had been killed. Looking about at the utter devastation and chaos left me with a feeling of profound awe and wonder that we had chosen to use the shelter and not remain at home as some of our neighbors had unfortunately done.

I lost some of my little friends that day and as a small lad of four, I was sad about that. But strangely, surrounded by all that human carnage and destruction, the overpowering emotion was not fear but a sense of security I did not understand.

The next night our family found a place to sleep in a local school that had opened its doors to the survivors of the latest bombing. And after a stint living with relatives, we finally located a rental house on the other side of town.

But there were other threats, other terrors awaiting, like the "flying doodlebugs"—unmanned German planes loaded with bombs that detonated upon impact, sending showers of shrapnel and sparks in all directions. I learned quickly, along with all the others, to dive for cover when the engines cut out. That silence could be fatal, for it meant not that the danger was past, but that the plane was plummeting at that very moment toward its next unsuspecting target.

Those early years of my life were painted in somber tones of black and white, relieved by occasional bold splashes of color provided by my mum. Even war could not suppress her high spirits; she kept some semblance of sanity in our lives with her stories and games. All four of us children continued to blossom under her nurturing care, much like the tender plants in her garden.

There were days when she allowed us to wander out among the tents pitched along the shore next to the docks near our home. Here were Allied troops. They had come over to form an invading army and would later occupy northern France before pushing their way toward Germany and the defeat of our enemies.

But on these leisurely afternoons, the Yank soldiers seemed amused by little Brits behaving like children everywhere. "Got any gum, chum?'' we would ask, and my brothers and I were rewarded frequently with the coveted strips of American chewing gum, unlike the hard, sugar-coated pellets we were accustomed to.

Always, come Sunday, we attended Sunday school and church, a warm and familiar ritual that evoked a deep sense of peace in those increasingly troubled times and held at bay the omnipresent specter of death.

At one Sunday night service held shortly after the bombing of our home, the church was packed with servicemen, all doubtless seeking solace from the war. The minister spoke words of encouragement and comfort but left us with a challenge in Jesus' own words: ''Behold I stand at the door, and knock: if any man hear my voice, and open the door, I will come in to him, and will sup with him, and he with me'' (Revelation 3:20, KJV). After that, he asked to see the hands of all who wished to invite Jesus to come into their hearts.

I put up my hand and, when the minister encouraged all inquirers to come down to the front, I asked permission from my parents and hurried down with many others.

The crowd in the vestry almost swallowed my small form, but the compassionate minister singled me out. ''I want to see this one in my office,'' he said, and led me in, where behind closed doors he heard my confession of faith and prayed with me. To be taken seriously by this kindly man of God was cause for rejoicing, and I left his office walking tall indeed.

Recuperating from my near-drowning, I lingered over this memory. Young as I was, a scant two months before my fifth birthday, I knew my initial experience with the Lord had been real. While other believers might someday reflect on ''foxhole conversions'' and question the validity of an experience fostered by the high emotion of wartime, I was much too young for this kind of complex reasoning. I had simply responded to the Voice within and opened the door of my heart to invite Him in.

When the war ended, the years skipped by swiftly. I recalled some doubts and temptations that marred my young manhood, but thought gratefully of my parents and an understanding pastor who had steered me safely through those perilous rites of passage. There was a further step of commitment to God around age fourteen, preceding a successful stint in a prestigious all-boys' school from which I was graduated.

Then, before I knew it, it was time for my military tour of duty, two years of "national service," as it was called in Britain. On the first night away from home, I made a hard decision. Dropping to my knees beside my bunk in the barracks, I had my devotions openly, choosing to make public my stand for Christ before the most critical audience possible, my peers. That decision stood me in good stead when I was shipped out to Kenya, Africa.

Again, the Lord's hand was upon me. Soon after arriving, I spent my first off-duty hours with some other military personnel in the home of John and Sophie Kitts, a British and American missionary team. They entertained homesick servicemen frequently, but their chief ministry was to prisoners, many of whom were savage Mau Mau tribesmen, convicted of everything from petty larceny to murder. It was John who introduced me to the special ministry of the Holy Spirit and shared deeply from the well of his personal experience in Spirit-led living.

I had been brought up to be wary of emotional "Pentecostal" experiences, but here was a man who radiated Christ. Because I could so clearly see the glory of God emanating from John, I deeply desired what he had, and returned home to England with a great hunger for God.

Within a few days I found myself in a revival meeting, standing out in the aisle with hands being laid on my head for the filling of the Holy Spirit. The revivalist shouted out the words of a prayer and pushed me hard on the forehead, forcing me back into the arms of an assistant who laid me flat on my back on the floor. I felt as cold as ice in the spirit and further from the Holy Spirit than I had ever felt in my life!

At one point I had weighed up these experiences. Which were genuine and which were false? All in all, I concluded that my salvation experience, while unspectacular, was authentic. On the other hand, my initiation into the "deeper life" was sadly disappointing. Yet I knew there was still lacking in me some vital ingredient, some passion I had observed in both John and Sophie. Truly they had responded to Paul's appeal to "offer your bodies as living sacrifices, holy and pleasing to God" (Romans 12:1).

Living sacrifices! I searched my soul. Was this the kind of "death" Christ meant when He spoke of dying to self? And how did one go about living sacrificially in a society that emphasizes success and self-fulfillment? I had pondered those deep thoughts long and hard, but without real resolution. For while I admired those godly friends, the idea of relinquishing my own goals and dreams was not very appealing. And as I left the service and pursued higher education, got married and became a father, the lofty spiritual ideals of my early days were buried beneath the weight of adult responsibilities.

My mind raced across the years to the more immediate past: 1973, Warminster, England. I was living the "good life" by all standards—comfortable home, loving wife and children, a position of great respect in the community as headmaster of St. John's Anglican School, and bright prospects for advancement in my field. Despite all this, I was at an all-time low.

Deep within, where it had been building over a period of several years, was a brooding restlessness and dissatisfaction. Though our family was active in a local evangelical church where I often served as lay preacher, I suspected that my disquietude stemmed from something deeper than disappointment with the institutional Church.

It bothered me, for example, that so many Christians seemed content with an appearance of Christianity while failing to demonstrate much real power in their lives. And where in *my* life was the evidence of Jesus' declaration "Whoever believes in me, as the Scripture has said, streams of living water will flow from within him" (John 7:38)? I saw little vitality, little real life. Instead of living water flowing out from us, our churches seemed to be mired in stagnant marshes.

This pot of internal unrest had come to a boiling point one summer Sunday morning. A statement made by the minister crystallized all the questions and doubts that had been taking shape for so long. It was a simple, basic truth, one that I myself had "preached" many times: "We really ought to love."

Was that our problem? Was the life being choked from our churches because we did not know how to love as God loves—unconditionally and sacrificially? And if so, what did I really know of that kind of love, that kind of abandonment to His purposes, anyway?

I thought of my mum and of my wife, Heather, to whom servanthood seemed to come so naturally. I thought of Sophie and John, the erudite British-American team, giving their lives away to primitive tribespeople in Africa. I thought of Jesus—the incarnate God, the King of kings and Lord of lords—emptying Himself of privilege and rank to die on a common cross for *me!*

Suddenly the message, right there in church, became painfully personal. How willing would I be to follow Him if the path led to a different destination from what I thought it would be? Would I insist on fighting for my own rights? Or would I abandon myself to the revealed and obvious will of the Lord, even if it meant submission to the point of death?

The scene of Jesus in Gethsemane came to mind. He had a struggle, unbelievably hard. I saw the picture Luke paints for us in his twenty-second chapter: Jesus in anguish of spirit, crying to His Father in heaven, "Father, if You are willing, take this cup from Me; yet not My will, but Yours be done."

It was not that I didn't want to live for others, nor that I didn't understand the principle. Surely no one could doubt my devotion to Heather and our three children. I would die for them! But would I do the same for others, for the Lord? The honest truth turned my blood cold. Oh, I could tell people how *they* ought to live, in eloquent sermons and pious prayers, but I could not do it myself!

No longer able to resolve the inner turmoil and overwhelming sense of my own hypocrisy, I stormed out of the church, vowing never to enter its doors again until I could experience for myself the dynamic transformation Jesus offers. Awash with fresh conviction, I knew that positive steps must be taken to remedy the whole question of hypocrisy in my life.

The Lord had already provided a time and place.

With the summer holiday upon us, we were looking forward to a complete change of scenery and environment. That year we would be staying in a farmhouse in the small Somerset village of Winsham, close to the beautiful seaside resort of Lyme Regis.

As the date of our departure drew near, I sensed an increasing desire to meet with God in a new, meaningful way. I felt sick at the thought of returning from that holiday to face another year of shallow Christian living. I was tired of secondhand sermons and theories about Jesus. I wanted to know *Him,* intimately and personally. I was like a dead man, spiritually numb. I needed resurrection!

The night before we left for the holiday, I poured out my heart to God in a desperate cry that came from the core of my being: "Lord, I will give up everything I have if You will give me the reality of Yourself. I am willing to give up being a headmaster. I'll even be a—a *dustman,* a garbage collector, if You will reveal Yourself to me!"

From that moment a great peace entered my heart. It was the assurance that God had heard and would respond.

The holiday was perfect in every way. We soaked in the beauties of the Somerset countryside. We swam in the sea and basked in the sun on the beach.

Then, while on a shopping trip to the nearby town of Chard, we noticed a flyer posted outside the town hall, advertising an interdenominational Bible study to be held that evening. Sensing a growing spiritual appetite in my son Andrew, who was then twelve, I persuaded him to accompany me.

I shall never forget my impressions upon entering the town hall that evening. The atmosphere was different from any religious gathering I had experienced. There emanated from the people a joy and peace and love that were electric in their authenticity. Faces glowed with the joy of the Lord, and when they spoke together, they looked into each other's eyes as if they had nothing to hide.

A spark of hope caught fire in my soul. Had I found what I was searching for here among these simple folk?

The Bible study was taken from Ezekiel 37, the great sermon delivered in the Valley of Dry Bones. As the Word of God was expounded upon with insight and clarity, I saw myself in that valley—a useless skeleton of a man, dried up, disjointed.

What could I achieve for Jesus Christ in that helpless state? I knew the answer: Absolutely nothing.

Then came the voice of the Lord to my heart: *Can these bones live?* I waited expectantly, barely able to draw a breath. The prophet Ezekiel answered for me: "Only You know that, Lord."

I could hardly believe it. This sermon was for me. It was as if all the others, including Andrew, had been swept away from sight and I alone waited before the Lord. God was speaking to *me!* Could I live again, or was I to remain forever in this dry, dead, useless state?

Prophesy upon these bones, I heard the Lord's words thunder through the stillness. *Say unto them, "O ye dry bones, hear the word of the Lord."*

I was literally sitting on the edge of my seat, perspiring with excitement. This was the Lord almighty speaking to me. I knew He was telling me He would speak to me again, and that I must pay careful attention to everything He would say.

Suddenly He spoke: *Behold, I will cause breath to enter into you, and ye shall live!*

Those words rang out like a trumpet blast from heaven and met an answering response from my heart. "Thank You, Lord! Now I know You mean business with me."

Andrew and I slipped out before the end of the meeting, and as we walked away from the town hall, we could hear the congregation singing praises to God. My spirit soared in unarticulated praises of my own. I would live! He had promised it!

The following morning was a Saturday. As I had to prepare the sermon for the little chapel at Bratton where I had a long-standing engagement to preach the next morning, I shut myself away in the bedroom of the farmhouse and opened my heart to the Lord in a new way.

I asked Him to show me what He wanted me to speak about,

with the condition that I did not want to preach anything that did not spring from personal experience or the practice of truths I had learned firsthand.

The Lord took me immediately to Romans 7, especially verses 18 and 19:

> I know that nothing good lives in me, that is, in my sinful nature. For I have the desire to do what is good, but I cannot carry it out. For what I do is not the good I want to do; no, the evil I do not want to do—this I keep on doing.

Yes, Lord, I recognize myself. As I read on to verse 24, I came to the words that expressed my feelings exactly as they were prior to the holiday: "What a wretched man I am! Who will rescue me from this body of death?"

The Lord was still speaking right down the line. He had my ear. I read on into chapter 8: "Therefore, there is now no condemnation for those who are in Christ Jesus, because through Christ Jesus the law of the Spirit of life set me free from the law of sin and death."

The whole of chapter 8 goes on to speak of the function of the Holy Spirit in giving us the power to live for Christ Jesus and as sons of God instead of being trapped in our sinful human natures. Key verses leaped from the page:

> Those who live in accordance with the Spirit have their minds set on what the Spirit desires. . . . The mind controlled by the Spirit is life and peace. . . . Those who are led by the Spirit of God are sons of God. . . . The Spirit himself testifies with our spirit that we are God's children. . . . The Spirit helps us in our weakness.
>
> verses 5, 6, 13, 16, 26

I was beginning to realize that without giving the "breath of God," the Holy Spirit, full access to my life, I would never know the reality and richness of the life of the Father and the Son. I would always remain a set of dry bones!

The following morning we traveled from our holiday home to the pretty village of Bratton, which nestles under the hills of the famous Westbury White Horse, so named because of the white chalk of the hillside.

The service was different from any I had ever conducted. There were neither eloquent prayers nor a polished sermon. Instead, for the first time in my life, I stood in the pulpit and simply told the truth. I apologized for sermons I had delivered on previous occasions, sermons that were not born out of practice, and I asked for prayer so that God would give me my heart's desire— to know Him as the early disciples knew Him, in daily moment-by-moment communion. That this knowledge would exact a great price from me did not occur to me at the time. If it had, I doubt that it would have deterred me, so earnest was I in my quest.

I shared with the congregation what I had learned from Romans 7 and 8 the previous day. I admitted to the people that I had not had the reality of a close relationship with Jesus as I had pretended. I told them that my deepest desire was to receive God's power so I could fulfill His plan and purpose in my life, wherever it led.

Instead of many worshipers pushing forward to greet me after the unusual service, only one young lady sought me out. She told me of an identical experience she had been living through and asked me to pray that she also would be given the true life of Jesus, through the outpouring of the Holy Spirit.

My family and I returned to the farmhouse in Winsham and retired. I was relieved that I had at least stripped away my mask and that there was no longer any need to play games with my fellow Christians.

About four in the morning, I woke up. I rubbed my eyes, thinking there was something wrong with my vision. There, on the bedroom wall in front of me, shimmering in silvery, luminous letters, was a text. It was similar to the farewell message that terminates a fireworks display.

Nudging Heather awake, I pointed to the wall. "Look!" I said in a loud whisper. "Look at those words!"

She sat up immediately and peered into the darkness. "What words? There's nothing there."

"You mean you can't see them?" I was incredulous. "Why, they are as clear as daylight to me. They read: 'IF YOU THEN, THOUGH YOU ARE EVIL, KNOW HOW TO GIVE GOOD GIFTS TO YOUR CHILDREN, HOW MUCH MORE WILL YOUR FATHER IN HEAVEN GIVE THE HOLY SPIRIT TO THOSE WHO ASK HIM?' " As I finished reading, the words faded away.

"That's wonderful!" Heather agreed sleepily. "And we've just been choosing gifts for the children's birthdays, too, haven't we?"

Indeed, we had just celebrated Andrew's birthday eight days previously, while Susan's was four days away. As is customary in most families, selecting an appropriate gift was an important part of the preparations. How precious of the Lord, I thought in amazement, to approach us so gently, giving us a modern-day parable.

The next morning, as soon as I awoke, I searched through the Bible for the verse I had seen on the wall the night before. I discovered the text in Luke 11:13, and went to bed that night with the warm assurance of God's presence.

Again, at four in the morning, I awoke to find shining letters on the wall ahead of me.

Wondering if Heather would be able to see them this time, I poked her. "Wake up, dear! There's another text on the wall!"

Heather struggled up blearily beside me.

"Look at those words," I said, pointing to the bright neon letters.

"I can't see anything. What does it say?"

Again I read the message aloud: "I WILL POUR OUT MY SPIRIT UPON ALL FLESH."

Heather sank back down into the snug bedclothes. I could sense that she was feeling a little cheated that she had not been able to see the message for herself.

Twice more the scenario was repeated. In the night I would awaken with a sense of God's peace and presence alive in the room. I would sit up in bed and discover the verse of Scripture before me. Then, wanting to share the experience with my wife, I would wake Heather who listened as I read the words: "ASK, AND YOU WILL RECEIVE" and "NOT BY MIGHT, NOR BY POWER BUT BY MY SPIRIT, SAYS THE LORD."

By now, Heather was losing interest in hearing a secondhand version of a miracle in the middle of the night. When, on the fifth consecutive night, I woke her to tell of yet another text on the wall, she merely sighed wearily and turned over. "What is it this time?"

"TARRY YE IN JERUSALEM."

"What!" she cried, sitting bolt upright in bed. "Jerusalem! You're not telling me that you're flying off to Jerusalem, are you?"

"No, no, my dear," I assured her, speaking soothingly. "The Lord is telling me to wait, just like the disciples had to wait before the Day of Pentecost."

That was the last time a verse appeared on the bedroom wall. But it was enough to change everything. I was learning that when

God's hand is on a life, He never lets go until that life is fully surrendered.

The cease-fire had been signed. My soul was "occupied territory." Now I was eager to enter another phase of my relationship with my Lord. How would He choose to communicate next time? And what would He have to say to me?

I knew it was only a matter of time before He confronted me again. This time I would be ready.

3
On the Mountaintop

"If you then, though you are evil, know how to give good gifts to your children, how much more will your Father in heaven give the Holy Spirit to those who ask him!"

Luke 11:13

Except for the ticking of the clock on the mantel, our house on Highbury Park was hushed and still. Upstairs, baby Tim was already sound asleep. With Heather and the two older children at a local cinema for the evening showing of a Walt Disney film, I was quite alone. And yet I was not alone. I was shut in with God.

The words of the Lord came to mind as clearly as when I had seen them written on the bedroom wall: "Ask, and you will receive." No promise could be simpler or clearer than that. It had been given by the mighty Lord God Himself, Creator of the universe, keeper of promises. I knew He was here with me now, gently reminding me that He is the God whose words are pure, like silver refined seven times. My sense of expectancy and excitement mounted. I wanted to be filled with God Himself.

So I simply asked Him for the gift He had promised.

To my surprise and delight, instead of some great and awesome manifestation of power such as a rushing wind or flaming tongues of fire, I experienced a beautiful fresh desire to praise Jesus. For the first time in my life I was able to say to Him, as if face to face, "I love You, Jesus. I love You, Lord, with all my heart." This freshness of true worship was like an inner spring of praise being released from within my spirit.

Suddenly the Lord brought to mind a person who had tried to show me a few years previously the importance of the Holy Spirit's ministry in the life of a believer. I had cut him short. Now the Lord brought his name to me—Derrick Maguire. I knew I must call him at once.

I got up from my knees and went straight to the telephone. I rang Derrick and told him that I was seeking the Lord in a new way, to receive the outpouring of His Holy Spirit, and asked him to pray for me. He agreed readily, mentioning that his family would join in prayer.

As I knelt again at the settee, I began to lift up my heart in praise to God. To the trickle of Living Water released within me, I added my own faltering words of love and praise. As I did this, I discovered that the flow increased from a trickle to a stream, and then built until it was like a roaring river. The desire to contribute more and more of my own words of sincere praise to the One who loved me so much that He died for me on a cross grew until a torrent of praise was rising to Him. I could not thank Him and praise Him and love Him enough for all that He had done for me!

I was discovering what a great difference there is between being able to worship God from the heart—that is, from one's innermost being—and to worship Him simply with head and intellect. I thought of all the years I had attended church since my childhood. I had participated in hundreds of worship services, had sung thousands of hymns. I had prayed publicly and privately, had even delivered sermons, but never had I felt such *reality* of true worship, such spiritual fulfillment, such a sense of the wonder of God's presence.

Now, in retrospect, I realized that most of the time I had not been worshiping God in truth. I had merely engaged in ritual, the trappings of religion. It was like getting into an automobile without gas. No matter how up-to-date the model, how complete the accessories, without fuel there can be no forward motion. My spiritual life was much like that—going nowhere because there was no real appropriation of power in my life.

Now there was no stopping the joyous expressions of my

praise. Nor did I want to stop! Strange sounds came to my lips, but these were not the softly chanted syllables of the Africans I had met during my military service in Kenya nor any other dialect I had ever heard. And though I had by now completed my formal academic training, I had never encountered in school anything that sounded quite like this. I was speaking fluently a language I had never learned. I knew only that I could open my mouth at will and pure unfettered praise flowed forth sometimes in English, sometimes in the new tongue.

Above all, I was aware that the sovereign God was right there in the room with me. He who was the object of all this praise and adoration was also its source. He had called me into His presence for sweet fellowship and was now giving me the words with which to communicate with Him. No effort on my part was required—no crafting of a sermon or prayer, no laboring over the well-turned phrase. For the first time in my life, I was conscious that the Lord was delighting in my worship, that it pleased Him tremendously. And I was able at last to satisfy the deepest yearnings of my heart—to worship Him "in spirit and in truth," purely, wholly, fully.

The changes that followed confirmed the reality of my encounter with the living Lord. Some of the changes were immediate and obvious; others, more subtle and gradual. Some were downright embarrassing.

Like the matter of my giving. I had always been as careful and as tight with money as any pauper on the streets. If I ever put a pound note in the offering bags, it was either because, by some oversight, I had spent the last coins in my pocket, or because I was sitting next to someone I wanted to impress with my generosity! Now I got out my checkbook and began making restitution to the Lord for all the money I owed Him. This desire was in itself a miracle.

The Word of God had already come alive in a dynamic way, but now it took on an even more significant role. Under the anointing of the Holy Spirit, it was the very voice of God to my heart.

One function of the Holy Spirit is to lead us in the pathway of truth. Like Jesus Himself, the Spirit is a teacher and instructs us in all we need to know to do God's perfect, holy will. This ministry of the Holy Spirit in teaching and revealing the very thoughts and words of God began to transform my life.

Not long after my encounter I was asked to preach at a large international church. Quite honored by the invitation, I sought the Lord earnestly about the message He wanted me to give.

As I prayed and studied the Word of God, the following question burned in my heart: "What shall it profit a man if he gain the whole world and lose his own soul?"

I began to suspect that God's profit and loss columns would look quite different from ours. Meditating on this Scripture, the Holy Spirit gave me a nudge. Could it be that I had all my priorities upside-down, that I had used the world's standard to establish my values? I had thought, for example, that preaching in this famous church was a great honor and a big step in my life.

Not at all, said the Lord. *If you want to take a big step up, go to Heather and promise her that you'll wash the dishes once a day—and don't forget to keep your promise!*

God was showing me that the "big things" in His estimation are almost the reverse of what the world would have us believe. Preaching a sermon in a famous church, holding an important office, writing a book—these are not the "big things." Nor is making it to the top of one's profession, earning a large salary or owning the finest house on the block. The "big things" in God's eyes are found in loving God and loving others as He loves us.

A bunch of flowers, a pat on the shoulder, a hug, a welcome-

home kiss, emptying the trash, offering a word of encouragement, showing love to others in a thousand ways—these are His
priorities, I was discovering. And saying, "Sorry, I was wrong,"
and, "I forgive you, let's forget it" are greater still.

Another way in which God began to teach me after I received
the outpouring of the Spirit was through dreams. When He wants
to underline some important principle from His Word, He often
gives a special dream that leaves a clear impression of the point
He wants to make. One such dream highlighted, of all unlikely
things, a bottle of fog!

In the dream I was shopping with my father. We had stopped
outside an old-fashioned chemist's shop, where all kinds of colorful liquids were displayed in the strangest assortment of bottles.
My father pointed at them and, with a twinkle in his eye, said,
"Let's play a joke, son! Let's go in and ask to purchase a bottle
of fog."

I knew my dad's sense of humor and started to chuckle. As I
began to picture the look on the shop assistant's face, my chuckle
turned to laughter, and soon I was rocking the bed in a fit of
merriment.

I returned to consciousness with Heather's voice calling in my
ear, "Darling, what on earth are you laughing at?"

Rubbing the sleep from my eyes, I pulled myself to a sitting
position, rearranged the pillows behind me and launched into a
description of the dream.

Heather was fully awake by now. "Bottle of fog?" she mused.
"That's strange. The next-door neighbor was saying only yesterday that too many people try to bottle God up within the limits
of their own mind. She's right. When we do that, all we have is
a bottle of fog, haven't we?"

I suppose that is the great difference between my former experience of the Lord Jesus and my present experience. Formerly

He was remote, impersonal, unattainable, much like a stained-glass window or a work of art. But now He had become a glorious reality, an intimate confidant who shared every area of my daily life. He was my Lord, my King, my Savior and my God, of course, but principally and by his own admission He was my Friend.

Friends enjoy being together, sharing the joys and the troubles and sorrows of life. A photograph of that friend, displayed on the mantel shelf, is not the same thing as having that person with you. My previous experience of Jesus was like having a picture of Him upon the mantel shelf of my mind. I knew a lot about Him, but I didn't know Him intimately. I knew virtually nothing of His willingness to give me clear guidance, to point out pitfalls and steer me with personal, explicit direction in every decision.

The most amazing thing about being called to be a friend of Jesus is that the relationship is divinely inspired, initiated by God the Father and maintained by the Holy Spirit. It is a love relationship of supernatural qualities. When the Lord pours out His Holy Spirit upon us in answer to our cry for reality, heaven comes down to earth and we bask in a love of new dimensions, a love that is pure, far-reaching and everlasting, a love that is the work of God.

Such love demands a response. And that response can only be reciprocal love if the relationship is to grow richer. Falling in love with Jesus is costly in terms of commitment and obedience, but the love relationship endures for all eternity. It is the fulfillment of God's purposes in creation and redemption.

Jesus said, "If anyone loves me, he will obey my teaching. My Father will love him, and we will come to him and make our home with him" (John 14:23). Obedience is both proof and product of our love for God.

Almost immediately after my encounter with the Lord of love,

He asked me to do some unusual things to test my willingness to obey Him. One thing He asked of me was that I go up to a wooded hill overlooking the heart of Warminster and pray for the town every day, early in the morning or late in the evening. Once I felt that the Lord was leading me to spend the whole night in prayer, interceding for the citizens of the town on the lonely hilltop.

On another occasion the Lord impressed me to sell our family car and give the money to the poor. At first I resisted, feeling that this was too extreme. Nor was I looking forward to mentioning it to Heather, who was still reeling from the chain of dramatic events since the first of September. I plucked up my courage, however, and broached the subject with her.

"Dear, I think the Lord is saying we don't need a car. Shall we try to sell it and give the proceeds to someone in need?"

Heather shot me a searching look. "Has the Lord told you to do it?"

"Well, yes, He has," I replied somewhat apologetically.

"Then we must do it." There was not a trace of doubt in her voice.

We thought the car was worth about three hundred pounds, and I arranged to have it serviced in order to get the best price. Shortly after delivering the car to the service engineer, he phoned me to say that he had discovered a dangerous crack in the chassis and that it was fit only for the scrap yard! Its worth was estimated at around forty pounds.

Heather and I were sorry that the Lord was only going to get forty pounds for the poor, but we were deeply grateful to Him for saving our family from a possible accident and far greater loss.

The Lord was showing me through this experience that obedience is always the best policy, since He alone knows what is best. Not only does He know every detail of every event occurring in my life and around the world, but He knows what is going to happen tomorrow. If He takes the trouble to tell us what He wants us to do, then He must have a special reason, and we are foolish if we disregard Him. I decided that when He spoke, I would just do it, and leave the results to Him.

When David wrote these beautiful words as the Holy Spirit gave inspiration, he was speaking for you and for me:

> Where can I go from your Spirit? Where can I flee from your presence? If I go up to the heavens, you are there; if I make my bed in the depths, you are there. If I rise on the wings of the dawn, if I settle on the far side of the sea, even there your hand will guide me, your right hand will hold me fast. . . . Your eyes saw my unformed body. All the days ordained for me were written in your book before one of them came to be. How precious to me are your thoughts, O God! How vast is the sum of them!
>
> Psalm 139:7–10, 16–17

One of the most striking changes that began to take place in my life was a lack of concern for my own reputation, and a great concern that the Lord would receive the credit for anything He did in our lives.

At the end of our summer vacation, I called a meeting at school and informed the teachers that, while I had always tried to run the school in the best interests of students and faculty, I had been primarily concerned for my own success and reputation. I told them that from that moment on, the Lord was going to be the director and would receive credit for any successes we might achieve. When the chairman of the board of managers, who was also the minister of St. John's Church, heard the story of my spiritual renewal, he was so impressed with the change in my attitude that he asked me to preach at the church and tell his congregation what had happened.

The concern I showed for my reputation used to put me under all kinds of emotional pressure in the effort to maintain or improve my image. When Jesus became central, my image went out the window. The only thing that mattered then was that Jesus be exalted. Since He plainly told us, "Apart from Me, you can do nothing," what had I to boast of?

Just as the early disciples were witnesses first in their own locality before going to the far corners of the earth, the Lord kept us eighteen months as His witnesses in Warminster before giving Heather and me a new assignment in February 1975. Those eighteen months were a special time of teaching, healing and preparation for the demanding work ahead. That the Lord was equipping us for service became more and more obvious as doors opened for witness in school, churches and open-air evangelism.

One Sunday morning I was preaching at our Warminster church on the "amazing grace" of God in allowing such sinful rebels as I to be cleansed and to receive freely His gift of forgiveness and new life. I turned to a passage of Scripture that makes it all so clear: "Therefore, if anyone is in Christ, he is a new creation; the old has gone, the new has come! . . . God was reconciling the world to himself in Christ, not counting men's sins against them" (2 Corinthians 5:17, 19).

I had just started reading the words "God made him who had no sin to be sin for us" when suddenly I saw in my mind's eye a picture of a cross with Jesus upon it, gazing up into the face of His Father. Just then a hand, raised in heaven, began to fall with mighty power upon the figure on the cross. The form of Jesus then changed into the ugliest, most vile and despicable-looking thing you could ever imagine. It was utterly repulsive. The hand from heaven struck that creature and it died.

I cried out, "Not Him! It is I who should be there!" In that moment the wonder of God's love and grace overwhelmed me, and tears filled my eyes for this precious Savior. "Hallelujah! Hallelujah! He did it for me!" I cried. "He did it for you so we might become the righteousness of God."

Day by day I was learning to live and minister in the power of the Holy Spirit and to abandon the strivings of the flesh. Only when the Spirit's anointing is upon a person is there real power to convict, to heal, to change. And it is only when we are in this place that we become His witnesses.

I discovered quickly that the enemy attacks the sincere seeker in subtle ways, principally in the area of the will. If he can get us to a point of frustration, unrelenting anger or resentment, he knows we will be powerless to witness Christ to others.

My joy in finding the reality of Jesus as a personal and intimate Friend in the early days became such an obsession with me that when Heather or one of the children interrupted my devotions, I would get upset and sometimes explode in frustration. On one occasion Heather was so troubled with this thoughtless reaction that she told me later she phoned Derrick Maguire's wife, Jean, and asked her to pray about the situation.

"Don't worry about it, Heather," Jean advised. "Ray is living on a mountaintop at the moment, but he'll soon come down. You'll have to help him keep his feet on the ground. Ring him up at school and tell him you love him."

And she did. What a great blessing it is to have a wife who is joined to me in a partnership where our aims, desires and destiny are the same. We were one in heart and one in the Lord from the beginning, but after our spiritual renewal—since hers was parallel to mine—our relationship was greatly enriched. My ministry was chiefly outside the home, while Heather's was inside the home, covering me in prayer. Each day became an adventure we began together, sharing God's Word and seeking His plan for our lives.

And so I went back to school, with the Lord Jesus Christ as my personal instructor. To my chagrin, I found that there was much remedial work to be done, and frequent assignments with periodic tests so I might know how I was getting on.

Slowly, as I was able to receive the truth, the Lord led me into a new place of servanthood. But like so many students I have known, I was easily sidetracked by some of the more provocative issues.

One of these was signs and wonders. The notion that God still operates supernaturally, breaking into the routine of our lives with healings and other wondrous works, intrigued me, and I applied myself diligently to my studies in this area. Still, a preoccupation with such things can divert us from the priority of being witnesses to our Lord Jesus through anointed words and consistent Christian living. Like Pliable, in Bunyan's *Pilgrim's Progress,* we can get trapped in the Slough of Despond and miss God's best for our lives.

Paul, writing to a church that was preoccupied with supernatural manifestations of the Spirit, said to them, "And now I will show you the most excellent way" (1 Corinthians 12:31). He then proceeded to teach the lesson of love, which is the greatest sign of Jesus' presence.

Still, it was important for me to understand that Jesus is the same yesterday, today and forever. If He could raise up a crippled man in Jerusalem on the Day of Pentecost, He can raise up a crippled lady in Chicago on Thanksgiving Day or a crippled child in Africa on Christmas Day. If He could heal a woman of a long-term affliction in Bible times, He can touch a woman in Warminster this very day!

Our family was soon to test this premise.

4
The Healing

O Lord my God,
I called to you for help
and you healed me.
O Lord, you brought me up from the grave;
you spared me from going down into the pit.

Psalm 30:2–3

In the fall of 1973 Heather became ill. Actually, she had not been well since the birth of our youngest child, Timothy, eighteen months earlier. I was worried about her.

Usually cheerful and energetic, my wife now dragged herself through the daily household chores, relying on Sue and Andrew to help in the kitchen and to relieve her when she was too tired to care for the baby.

Life had not always been an endurance test. When I met Heather for the first time in 1956, she was glowing with good health. Wearing a pale blue satin and lace dress at her sister's wedding, and flushed with excitement and the warm September sun, she made a stunning first impression. All during the ceremony and the reception that followed, I could not take my eyes off her, making it difficult to attend to my duties as photographer for the festive occasion!

There was more to Heather's glow than good health and high spirits. Almost at once I discerned a sweetness of spirit that could have come only from the Lord Himself. And when I encountered her quite unexpectedly a few days later in a local shopping center, my heart leaped. The response I read in her dark eyes confirmed my own belief that God had truly brought us together. We were married two years later.

When Susan Joy arrived on our first anniversary, followed in two years by Andrew, we thanked the Lord for His blessing on our union. After a while it seemed there might be no more children, though Sue and Andrew pleaded for a little brother or sister. And when, eleven years later, we learned that we were to be parents again, we were surprised and delighted. Still, the pregnancy was complicated by toxemia, and only a miraculous stabilizing of Heather's blood pressure at the last minute enabled her to deliver Timothy naturally.

Baby Tim snuggled quickly into a warm place in each of our hearts. Susan doted on the new baby, and Andrew was pleased to have a little brother at last. My parents came down often to get acquainted with the latest grandson and to help out. So while Heather was weak and easily fatigued, there were always willing hands. I, of course, was caught up in my own duties—routine school affairs, meetings, reports.

The days passed in a blur of activity. Because Heather never complained, I suppose it was easy to pretend she was getting better.

And now, with our dynamic new relationship with the Lord, we were hearing from Him regularly. We approached our daily Bible readings with as much excitement as lovers awaiting a long-expected letter from the beloved. And that is precisely what it was. Each passage was a personal communiqué from the Lover of our souls. And just as one reads a love letter, slowly savoring every word, finding all the nuances of rich meaning that might be obscured from the eyes of a casual reader, so Heather and I devoured our Lord's words to us—sometimes admonishing, sometimes tender and comforting, sometimes startlingly direct.

More and more these ''messages'' began to assume a pattern. We were both struck by the number of references to ''the poor and needy,'' ''the fatherless,'' ''large cities'' and ''children.''

With my professional background and Heather's pre-school teaching experience and natural love for children, we began to believe that God might be preparing us to move to one of the large industrial cities in our country, probably Birmingham or

Manchester, perhaps to teach immigrants in an inner-city area. From the verses the Lord was giving us, this direction seemed fairly obvious.

A few days after Christmas, however, we received a telephone call that changed everything. The voice on the other end of the line belonged to a member of the Church of England community of St. Denys.

"I have a rather unusual message to deliver," she said. "I don't mind telling you I can't make anything out of it, but I'm sure it must have special significance for you."

We were intrigued and made an appointment for her to come share what God had shown her.

"The Lord awakened me in the night," she said when she arrived and the three of us were seated comfortably in the lounge. "I saw a clear picture of both of you." Her eyes widened. "Above your heads was the number 1165. Does that mean anything to you?" She looked inquiringly from one to the other.

"Absolutely nothing," I said, turning to Heather. "What about you, dear?"

"Afraid not." Then, brightening, she leaned forward. "Perhaps it is a Scripture reference—Psalm 116:5 or 2 Kings 6:5."

I picked up a Bible and turned the pages. Finding the passages, I read them aloud. But God was not speaking to me in those verses.

We saw our friend to the door and thanked her for coming. She left after promising to pray that the Lord would reveal the meaning to us. Then Heather and I played some more guessing games. Puzzled, we decided to wait upon the Lord and ask Him to show us if He had any purpose in sending that number.

Five weeks went by before we had a clue as to what the Lord might be doing.

On February 3, 1974, I awakened at about five o'clock in the morning with a mental picture of a hymnboard. In the center of that hymnboard was one hymn, number 1165! Hurrying downstairs, I looked it up in a large anthology, *Sacred Songs and Solos,* then mounted the stairs and entered our bedroom.

"Heather," I said, my voice betraying my excitement, "I've found it!" Then I proceeded to read the words to her:

> Come to the Savior, make no delay.
> Here in His Word, He has shown us the way.
> Here in our midst, He's standing today,
> Tenderly saying, "Come!"

We had sung this hymn often as children and loved it, but it held no particular significance on that Sunday morning. In my diary for that day, I wrote: "We leave it now in the Lord's hands. It could have been a flash of light into the future, but we must keep our eyes on the present."

It was another month before we were finally able to decode the message.

In mid-March our annual missionary conference was scheduled at Warminster Baptist Church. Heather stayed home with Tim on the Sunday evening when the Reverend David Martin, a missionary from Brazil, was to be the speaker.

In the vestry before the service began, I was asked to lead in prayer. "Lord," I prayed, "You said, 'All power is given unto Me. Go ye into all the world and preach the Gospel.' Bless Your servant tonight as he acts in obedience to that word."

To my amazement, after we left the vestry and took up our places in the church, the choir rose and began to sing the same words I had just prayed in my prayer of committal:

> All power is given unto Me.
> Go ye into all the world and preach the Gospel,
> And lo, I am with you always.

I could not believe my ears! It was as if God was echoing my prayer back to me as His own personal command to my heart. I had no doubt that the Lord was speaking as clearly as when He had written in shining letters on our bedroom wall.

The Reverend Martin's sermon text was Luke 12:48: Much is required from those to whom much is given. More is required from those to whom much more is given.

Once again, I was astounded. Only that afternoon I had been studying that very passage. The Lord had first pointed out Luke 9:60: "Your duty is to come and preach the coming of the Kingdom of God to all the world" (LB), then directed my attention to Luke 12:47: "Though he knew his duty, he refused to do it" (LB). It seemed more than coincidence.

As I meditated on the text, I realized that much had been given to me—a wife whom I loved and who loved me, three fine children, a comfortable home, a job with excellent prospects and provision for my every need. Above all, I had the Lord Jesus, with whom I was now enjoying the richest fellowship of my entire life as a Christian.

But now the Lord was saying that much would be required of me! What was He going to ask? Would I be willing to do it? Or would I be like the man in Luke 12:47 who refused to do his duty?

At the end of the service, I had a chat with David Martin. I told him that Heather and I felt we were coming to a crossroads in our lives. He questioned me briefly.

"And what is your work?"

I told him and mentioned that Heather and I both felt the Lord might be bringing us to a place of deeper involvement with children, possibly in a big city or in a residential school.

"Had you heard that the mission is looking for a couple to go to Sao Paulo in Brazil to care for the children of missionaries?"

The warm tingle that coursed through my body at his question had the effect of a mild electric shock. "No," I replied thoughtfully, "but it is obviously something Heather and I should pray over."

On the way home, I considered David Martin's words. Could the Lord really be asking us to go to Brazil? What about Heather's health? She was still far from well, despite the promise she felt God had given her that He would restore her. It was one thing to move to another city in Britain, but quite another to go to a faraway country about which we knew virtually nothing.

Arriving home, I let myself in. Without waiting to take off my coat, I went straight into the lounge, where I found Heather reading.

"Darling!" I exclaimed as I burst into the room. "I have just learned that the Baptist mission is looking for a volunteer couple to look after the children of missionaries in Sao Paulo, Brazil."

Glancing up from the book she was reading, she gave me a look of intense interest. "I think this is it! I really do! Everything fits. I believe it's for us."

For a moment I was stunned. That statement was as unlike Heather as bananas growing on a blackcurrant bush! She never made a major decision without considerable thought and prayer, and always gave weighty consideration to the negative aspects of any proposition.

"Well," I said, drawing a deep breath. "At least I intend to do some research."

In the family library I drew out an encyclopedia in which I located Sao Paulo and then rejoined Heather. "The largest city in South America," I read silently, "Sao Paulo boasts large communities of immigrants from all over the world. With this melting-pot mix, there are serious social and economic problems—among these, slum-dwellers."

As I was reading the details, Heather looked up with an expression of awe on her face. "You'll never guess what's here on the very next page I turned."

"What is it?"

"Hymn 1165, 'Come to the Savior'! It's quoted here at the top of the page!" She was almost squealing with excitement.

This time the meaning of the words struck us full-force:

Come to the Savior—We knew He had been calling us for some time to a deeper relationship with Himself.

Make no delay—A prompt response on our part was in order.

Here in His Word He has shown us the way—Yes, the Scriptures the Lord had been pointing out were leading us to this climactic moment.

Here in our midst He's standing today—His presence was very real as we realized how personal He was making this call.

Tenderly saying, "Come"—How could we refuse that gentle invitation?

The pieces were falling into place. In a remarkable way the Lord was confirming all the Scriptures He had given us.

Holding hands on the settee, we sat in stunned silence.

Finally I murmured a prayer: "Lord, if this is what You want, then we'll go. But please make it very clear to us when we should write and offer ourselves for this work."

"But my dear," Heather interrupted. "The song says, 'Make no delay!' "

I looked at her in surprise. "Are you saying I should write at once then, in spite of your illness?"

"I think those words *Make no delay* are important," she insisted.

I sighed deeply. "The Lord has certainly made things very clear up to now," I admitted. "But I would like further confirmation that He wants us to apply immediately. I'm going to ask

Him for another sign." I bowed my head once more. "If we should write to the mission right away, then please let South America be mentioned on the radio news broadcast that follows the half-hour hymn program."

We turned on the radio and listened, holding our breath. Was this being immature? Would the Lord respond to such a small request?

We hadn't long to wait. The notes of the melody drifted through the room, the words firm and unmistakably clear:

> O Master, when Thou callest,
> No voice may say Thee nay,
> For blest are they that follow
> Where Thou dost lead the way.

That song in itself was positive confirmation of God's call that evening, but when the news headlines were given and included the scores of a cricket match in Guyana, South America, we knew a letter had to be posted to the mission.

In the letter we stated all the facts of our call and gave a candid account of Heather's physical condition, adding that we believed that in God's time, she would be fit to assume the duties of housemother.

As I wrote I think I believed that by acting in obedience to God's call, the Lord would begin to heal Heather. On the contrary, she became worse. Most of our relatives thought we had been afflicted with religious mania to go on insisting that the Lord was going to heal her rather than consult a physician.

Then we remembered a vivid dream Heather had had months before in which she was looking through a hospital window into an operating theatre. She could see herself lying on the operating table with the surgeon bending over her. "There is nothing more we can do for her," he said, shaking his head. As the dream progressed, however, she was shown that the Lord Himself would heal her completely. Some time later the identical dream recurred. She wanted to wait about seeing a doctor and I felt it was important to honor her faith by supporting her.

Meanwhile, the mission wrote back that they would look forward to hearing from us when Heather's health returned. Thus, we began a time of waiting.

On Timothy's second birthday, Heather was feeling particularly weak and ill. In desperation she cried out to the Lord, "Have You forgotten Your promise, Lord?"

Turning to the Living Bible, she opened it at random. Her eyes fell on the fifteenth verse of Isaiah 49: *"Never!"* she read. "Can a mother forget her little child and not have love for her own son? Yet even if that should be, *I will not forget you.* See, I have tattooed your name upon my palm."

Despite the decline in Heather's health after our call to Brazil in March 1974, her faith that God would give her a complete and permanent healing never wavered. Even I was amazed at her certainty.

This was especially ironic in view of the fact that she was now only skin and bones, and growing more frail all the time. When she was on a rare outing with the family, I studied her gaunt features with mounting horror. She seemed to be fading away before my eyes and for the first time I gave way to tears, weeping openly and crying out to the Lord to spare her life.

I was profoundly relieved when Heather phoned me one day at school to say she knew the time had arrived to consult a physician. A friend had called and left a leaflet with the word *international* inscribed on it. She remembered she had seen this word in her special dream and felt it signified that it was time to act. We made an appointment with the consultant surgeon in St. Martin's Hospital, a large medical facility in the nearby town of

Bath. When the surgeon examined Heather, he diagnosed her condition as a large "bowler hat" ovarian cyst and scheduled major surgery almost immediately.

Flabbergasted at the news, I went upstairs and threw myself across the bed. "Where is Your healing, Lord? How can we go to Brazil if we are to wait for Heather's recovery from such an operation?"

That same evening the weekly church prayer meeting was to convene in our home. My faith shaken, I had little spiritual energy for such a meeting and was tempted to call the minister and ask him to change the venue.

As our friends arrived and learned about the operation, they seemed pleased that at last something was to be done about Heather's condition. But I felt sick at heart and found it difficult to sing the opening song.

Moving woodenly through the evening prayers and praise, I gradually felt a thawing in my spirit. The warmth grew until it suffused my entire being. So this was the meaning of "a sacrifice of praise"? I had seen the phrase in a chorus many times before. As I offered the Lord my worship as best I could in the face of the dark trial ahead, I experienced His presence in a new dimension.

Perhaps it is precisely when we cannot see the silver lining to the cloud or trace the rainbow through the rain that our praise takes on a special quality in God's sight. Surely this kind of sacrificial praise rings true with God and demonstrates, as nothing else can, that we love and trust Him even when we have not the least idea what He is doing in our lives.

As Heather and I offered up our praise to the Lord, committing the hospital appointment to Him, we found peace returning to our hearts. And when the pastor began reading from Romans 11, that peace passed all human understanding: "For God's gifts and his call can never be withdrawn; he will never go back on his promises'' (verse 29, LB).

Suddenly a glorious rainbow shone across the darkness that had almost obliterated the light of God's plan for us. Heather and I looked up simultaneously, our eyes meeting and locking in the strength of that reminder.

A few days later our good friend John Kitts, the missionary whom I had met as a young man in Kenya, arrived for some speaking engagements.

"We're looking for a miracle in your life, aren't we, Heather?" he asked as soon as he had greeted her.

"Yes, John. The Lord has promised that He is going to heal me."

Without further preliminaries, John placed his hands gently on Heather's head. "We thank You, Father, for the miracle You have promised to do in Heather's life. In Jesus' name, Amen."

That was all. Just a simple acceptance of God's promised gift of healing.

Nothing happened immediately. But during the night Heather felt a burning sensation working its way through her entire body. By morning the intense heat had subsided, and she knew she was healed.

At breakfast, John joined us for a special session of praise and thanksgiving in our family prayers. Now Heather was faced with an awkward situation. She knew the Lord had healed her, yet she was to be admitted to the hospital in a few days for surgery. What was she to do?

After prayer, she felt the Lord directing her to go through normal channels of hospital admission and trust Him to work things out in His way. Following that divine leading, I drove her to Bath and saw her safely into the surgical ward of the hospital.

When I visited her later that evening, she told me she had been examined by a doctor during the day. After giving her a thorough examination and double-checking the patient's notes, he had turned to her and asked, "What is your name and why are you here?"

Thus verifying that he had the right patient, he called in a second doctor, a woman, who also examined Heather thoroughly. This doctor confirmed that there appeared to be nothing wrong. "But," she said, "the specialist doesn't make mistakes. You will go down to the operating theatre tomorrow as scheduled."

"And are you going?" I asked her later.

"Oh, yes, the Lord is in complete control. He knows what He's doing." Heather seemed perfectly confident.

All the following day at school, I was restless. "Why, Lord?" I kept asking. "Why should Heather have to go through surgery just for the doctors to find that there is nothing there?"

At the end of the school day, I rang the hospital and asked about Heather's condition. "You can come and visit her as soon as you like," I was told. That journey to Bath was the longest eighteen miles of my life!

I parked the car and ran to the ward. There was Heather sitting up in bed. Aside from looking a little flushed, she appeared to be fine.

"What happened?" I asked.

"Well," she replied, smiling, "I had the anesthetic, went down to the theatre, and knew nothing more until I started coming 'round here in this bed. The first thing I did was feel my tummy to see if there were any stitches. There was nothing!"

"Praise the Lord!"

"Yes, that's what I said, too." She laughed. "Then I looked up and saw the surgeon standing at the foot of my bed, staring at me. I was curious to know why he hadn't operated.

" 'You may well ask,' he said, looking at me with something

akin to awe. 'Your whole body is in a state of healing. You have everything to be thankful for. You may go home tomorrow.' ''

To make certain that there was no growth or blockage in the lower digestive tract, Heather was called back a week later for further X rays. With a clean bill of health, we were ready to begin the process toward our acceptance for service in Brazil.

Yes, I have discovered, God does speak today and reveal His plans to those who are His children and learn to abandon themselves to Him. By His Word and by His Spirit operating in many ways, He guides supernaturally into preordained paths.

The enduring quality of the Word of God, under the anointing of His Holy Spirit, is its power. Ordinary words in the Bible are transformed into living messages from the mouth of God to a human heart. Such words have not only the capacity for changing the course of human life, but the destinies of nations.

But there must be listening ears on earth. If ever there was a need for people to have their ears open to the voice of the Lord, surely it is today. Every Christian, every servant of God and every proclaimer of good tidings should be daily repeating to the lost world and to our sleeping brothers and sisters in Christ: ''Hear the Word of the Lord!''

Before we could proclaim that Word to the lost in foreign lands, Heather and I first had to listen.

5
Lifeline

"Call to me
and I will answer you
and tell you great and
unsearchable things
you do not know."
                    Jeremiah 33:3

Prayer, for the Christian, should be as natural as breathing. But it was not always so for me. In fact, prayer used to be one of the dullest and most frustrating exercises of my life. I knew that God wanted fellowship with me and expected me to communicate with Him, but I had little confidence that He was paying attention when I did.

Technically, of course, I understood the concept of communication. I had taught it many times in my classrooms. Communication is the interchange of thoughts, feelings and information between two parties, the sender and the receiver. In communicating with God, I attempted to send messages that rarely seemed to get past the ceiling. And when I occasionally made a connection, it appeared to me that He was often too busy to return my call!

After I experienced the outpouring of the Holy Spirit in 1973, I learned that prayer is not simply talking to God or even engaging in a two-way conversation with Him, but rather *living in the presence of God*. In those divine encounters I was personally introduced by the Holy Spirit to the Lord Jesus and, through Him, ushered into the throne room of the King of kings.

I know a man who was, for a number of years, a member of the royal court of our greatly beloved Queen Elizabeth II. He tells me that one must observe a strict protocol when granted an audience with the Queen at Buckingham Palace.

The guest must never initiate a conversation, but must wait until spoken to. When addressed, one's first reply must be terminated with the words *Your Majesty,* and subsequent statements by *Ma'am.* In spite of the great affection with which we hold the Queen, such an audience can be a formidable experience.

What a contrast is our entry into the throne room of heaven! We can come into the presence of the King of kings with the same simplicity of a little child who climbs up onto his father's knee and gives him a hug. We can talk to God in our everyday language, expressing our love and gratitude, and yet also broaching any subject that concerns us. Or we can simply sit at His feet and wait for Him to speak to us. He Himself says, "If anyone hears me calling him and opens the door, I will come in and fellowship with him and he with me" (Revelation 3:20, LB).

Such an experience transcends mere words. Prayer thus became, for me, a heavenly exchange, the means by which I could touch the Father heart of God.

The move to South America with our three children was saturated in this new kind of prayer. Not only had God called us to a place; He had called us to a purpose—to die daily to our own ambitions and to find joy in glorifying Him. Following Him as He unfolded His customized plan for us was an adventure.

On arrival in Brazil in February 1975, we were sent by the mission to study Portuguese at a language school in Curitiba, capital city of the southern state of Parana. We had been there only a few weeks when a tragedy occurred at the Sao Paulo hostel 429 kilometers away.

The housemother, Lottie Parsons, a veteran missionary who was due to retire with her husband, Clifford, when they handed over the hostel to us in a year's time, had a sudden heart attack and died.

Panic almost overtook us when Heather and I realized that we were now expected to run the hostel. How could we take responsibility for such a project when we barely knew enough Portuguese to go shopping? Nor would we be able to navigate the confusing and dangerous streets of this largest city of South America with little or no knowledge of Brazilian customs and traffic laws. We had been told, too, to be wary of thieves who ply their trade in broad daylight.

Prayer became our lifeline. Aided by Clifford Parsons, who stayed with us for a month to ease the transition, we discovered our prayer times to be a powerhouse of faith and confidence that fueled our ventures into the streets.

On my first trip out alone, I found myself surrounded by crowds of busy shoppers, all speaking Portuguese so swiftly I could barely catch an intelligible word. I stood gazing in bewilderment at the concrete jungle, its skyline thrust against the burning blue sky, when my eye fell on a bright neon sign: AMORA. My heart leaped in recognition. That was one Portuguese word I knew! It meant "mulberry." Back in England, the Lord had spoken dramatically to me one day about mulberries: "When you hear the sound of marching in the tops of the mulberry trees, that is the time to attack" (see 2 Samuel 5:24). Now a warm glow filled me, and I thanked Him for this reminder that He knew the language and the customs and the traffic laws, and would help me.

Nevertheless, it was with keen relief that I made my way through the maze of streets and finally arrived back at the house that was to be our home in Sao Paulo.

The hostel was a large, split-level dwelling built on the side of a hill, with living accommodations on the upper floor and additional bedrooms in the basement for a total of twenty people. Like its neighboring properties, it was protected by high fencing and wooden window shutters. A roof jutting over the frontage acted as a carport.

As is true in many of the suburbs of Sao Paulo, the juxtaposition of extreme wealth and poverty was the case here as well. The condition of our neighbors across the street was appalling, and our hearts were moved to see little children in tattered shorts or dresses coming to our high front gate to beg for food.

Inside the hostel, life was hectic. The day started early; Heather and I rose at 5:30. The seven older children—five of them sons and daughters of missionaries—had to leave for school by 7:20 A.M., and Tim had to be in nursery school by eight. Heather's life was a merry-go-round of cleaning, cooking, ironing and tidying up in order to be ready to care for the children again after school.

When they arrived around four o'clock in the afternoon, the place was a beehive of activity—football, handball and tennis in the backyard on sunny days, and arranging stamp collections indoors if the weather was uncooperative. Homework always took priority, of course. And so the days flew by.

Sometimes, in the course of our busy lives, we are caught off-guard by the ferocity of an attack by the enemy. It is not surprising that Satan concentrates so much effort on preventing Christians from praying. He sends out his agents daily to persuade believers that they do not have time to shut themselves away, as Jesus commanded, to meet the Father face to face. Satan accuses us of wasting time, of being too heavenly minded, of neglecting other duties or persons in our lives, until we sometimes capitulate, drowning out the gentler pleadings of the Holy Spirit.

And sometimes, even when we are prayerful, we run into difficulty because a problem is too big for us to handle alone or because we give in to selfishness or resentment. At such times the Lord is gracious to send reinforcements.

While in Sao Paulo, an incident occurred that clearly illustrates the strength of corporate prayer.

One day, while walking through the busy shopping center of the city with twelve-year-old Jonnie in our care, I saw a slightly built man rushing straight toward me. When he was a couple of meters away, he dipped his shoulder and lunged into the pit of my stomach.

I collapsed onto the pavement, the wind knocked out of me. From the wrenching pain, I wondered if he had cracked some of my ribs. As I struggled to regain my breath, I suddenly remembered the money I had just withdrawn from the bank. I felt my side pocket. It was empty! Four hundred American dollars' worth of *cruzeiros* . . . gone!

A bystander who had seen the whole thing recreated the scene. While the first man was hitting me in the stomach, a second was behind me, grabbing the contents of my pocket and making an equally fast getaway through the crowded streets.

I was shattered! It wasn't the money that was so important, but the fact that it had been given sacrificially by a dear friend toward the price of a car, which we needed desperately. It seemed to me that the Lord had given, and the devil had taken away!

When I had recovered, Jonnie and I started out in the direction of the Evangelical Library, run by our friends Bill and Mary Barkley. They would help. Also our son Andrew was there. As soon as Andrew heard my story, he spread the word to other Christians working in nearby offices. Within half an hour, a prayer meeting was being held just a couple of hundred meters from the spot where the robbery had taken place.

A young Brazilian woman, Sueli, prayed that, through the robbery, the Lord would bring blessing and even multiply the sacrificial gift. At the time I thought this an impossible prayer, but quickly forgot it in the press of the other well-wishers who flocked by to shake my hand and tell me they would be praying for me.

By the time I reached home and was reunited with Heather and the rest of the family, I was able to count my blessings, among them the fact that I had not been seriously injured. I was also greatly encouraged and more than a little amused at the Lord's sense of humor when I picked up my Bible and opened it at random to read:

> We are pressed on every side by troubles, but not crushed and broken. We are perplexed because we don't know why things happen as they do, but we don't give up and quit. We are hunted down, but God never abandons us. We get knocked down, but we get up again and keep going.
>
> 2 Corinthians 4:8–9, LB

At family prayers that evening, we were able to offer true thanks and praise for what the Lord had accomplished. When it came Jonnie's turn to pray, his prayer was disarming in its honest appraisal of the situation: "Lord," he prayed, "You wanted to test Mr. Saunders to see if he really believed You were in control, or whether he would mope around and blame himself!"

The conclusion to the story is that Sueli's "impossible" prayer was wonderfully answered. When our Sao Paulo friends heard about the robbery, they sent generous donations toward the needed car. Within ten days the Lord had multiplied the original gift to eight hundred American dollars! We could not only purchase the vehicle, but pay the road tax and insurance and return to the Lord the tithe on the amount He had given us.

And I was assured that God will supply our needs if we keep His Kingdom as our first priority. We do not have to beg or plead for the essentials of life, but He does test us on occasion to see if we are prepared to wait for His timing for their arrival.

*   *   *

In January 1976, just after my near-drowning experience in Suarao, we were beginning to feel uneasy about remaining in the hostel work. Heather and I were growing increasingly disturbed by the numbers of children begging for food and the sharp contrast between rich and poor in the city.

Those early Scriptures that had branded my spirit and led to our call to mission service now blazed to new life: "Defend the cause of the weak and fatherless; maintain the rights of the poor and oppressed. Rescue the weak and needy" (Psalm 82:3–4). Jesus seemed to be saying again, "Let the little children come to me, and do not hinder them, for the kingdom of heaven belongs to such as these" (Matthew 19:14). And most conclusive of all was the strong word of the Lord in the book of James: "Religion that God our Father accepts as pure and faultless is this: to look after orphans and widows in their distress and to keep oneself from being polluted by the world" (1:27).

Had we followed Him fully in coming to care for the missionaries' children, or was God reissuing His first call?

One dark night, in the midst of a torrential downpour, the front bell of the hostel rang. I opened the upper windows of our living room and peered through the misty orange light of the street lamps. Down below, huddled next to the gate post, I could see two shivering forms. Assuming they were beggars, I took down the customary biscuits and oranges.

"Here you are," I said, passing the food through the metal railings of the gate. I could now see that the two dripping figures were mere boys—one, a dark-faced lad of about eight, the other, fair-skinned and slightly taller.

"Please, sir," asked the taller one. "Could we come in and shelter under your carport?"

I looked at the pouring rain and the river of water racing along the gutters. "Of course," I replied, opening the gate wide. "Come in and wait until the storm dies down."

As soon as Heather learned of the unexpected visitors below, she made two cups of steaming hot cocoa and carried them down to the grateful youngsters.

"When you finish your drinks and the rain stops, leave your cups inside the gate," I said, and told them goodnight.

Heather and I then retired to our quarters, assuming that in the morning we would find the two empty beakers on the tile floor of the carport.

But when I went down just after six o'clock the next morning, there were the two boys, sound asleep, stretched out on the cold tiles alongside the mission vehicle. The poor fellows were snuggled close to each other, sharing what little heat they could find against the chill of the damp early morning air.

I called to Heather.

Her eyes widened in surprise when she saw the boys. "Why didn't they go home?" she whispered. "What do you suppose they are up to?"

When they stirred, balling dirty fists into their eyes, I posed this question to them in Portuguese.

"Home?" asked the older boy. "We don't have no home. We live on the streets."

"But when did you last see your mother?" I asked.

"Oh, 'bout two years ago. She told me she couldn't look after me no more, that I'd have to do it myself. I met my friend here, so we look out for each other now."

I could see the horror in Heather's eyes as the awful realization dawned that we had just had our first encounter with abandoned children. But what about all those other children who had been coming to beg for food at our gate? Were they also homeless and abandoned?

We began to question neighbors and missionary colleagues. "Why, of course," they said, eyeing us curiously. "You mean you didn't know that there are thousands of children like that on the streets of Sao Paulo? They sleep under the viaducts, in the parks, in shop doorways, wherever they can find a warm, dry spot!"

We now knew without doubt why the Lord had brought us here. It was not to care permanently for the children of missionaries, but to reach out in love to children who did not know the meaning of the word.

With this realization, the Lord's teaching about abandonment took on new meaning for me. He had shown me that I must divest myself of all self-will in order to be truly abandoned to Him. Now I saw more clearly that only as I gave myself up for Him would I be able to give myself in service to Him. Seeing Him as Lord of those abandoned children gave me a renewed desire for Him to be Lord of my abandoned life.

We began to pray for guidance and enlightenment. What would be the next step?

Almost immediately the Lord gave me a vivid dream. In the dream I was traveling by bus on a circular route, with my destination about halfway around. When we came to my bus stop, however, I was not able to reach the exit because of the crowded gangway. I rang the bell repeatedly, but the driver ignored me and we sailed right past.

Finally noticing my frustration, the driver called to me: "Don't worry, friend. All you have to do is return to the base and catch a bus going directly to your destination. You can't miss it then!"

I awoke suddenly, my heart pounding with the thrill of revelation. We must return to England as soon as possible and prepare ourselves to work among these children in Sao Paulo.

Back in England, after only a year and a half in Brazil, we

approached the Baptist Mission Board hoping they would be able to fund a new work with orphaned and abandoned children. While they made it possible for us to travel to the supporting British churches to share the burden the Lord had placed on our hearts, it soon became clear that they would not be able to initiate a work of this nature.

We were thrown back on the Lord alone to show us the way. Praying as we had never prayed before, we asked everyone we knew who was a believer in prayer to join with us for direction.

The Word was full of encouragement: "If you remain in me and my words remain in you, ask whatever you wish, and it will be given you" (John 15:7). "He will call upon me, and I will answer him" (Psalm 91:15). There was no doubt in our minds that we would eventually hear from Him. He had promised.

It was almost a year later before we heard that our dear friend John Kitts was coming to Britain for a conference. Since John had been the Lord's instrument in our instruction and guidance so many times before, we looked forward to seeing him again. Perhaps he could shed some light on our latest need.

During that summer conference at which both Heather and I had been invited to speak, we experienced a breakthrough. One evening, after showing some slides of the children of Sao Paulo, Heather was approached by a well-dressed woman who told her that the Lord had spoken to her about us. Though the woman did not relate what the Lord had said, she did ask Heather about our plans to return to Brazil. The following day, she informed us that she had been led to pay the airfare back to Brazil for our entire family.

We were overwhelmed! Not only did the Lord answer our prayers for funds, but we believed that, according to eternity's values, something even more significant happened that week.

In the course of the conference, we met many people who

committed themselves to pray for us regularly. One of these, Violet Ponnuthurai from Sri Lanka, was an elderly prayer warrior whose powerful prayers undergirded us for years. In fact, we are convinced that much of what has been accomplished in our lives is due to the prayers of dedicated intercessors like Violet.

When the Spirit of God calls a person to pray for someone and that person is obedient and faithful, God releases His blessings in response. I cannot explain why He chooses to link His divine energy with that of His creatures. I know only that without intercessors—those who plead or petition on behalf of others—God will not act in some situations.

I feel quite sure that one of those situations was my near-drowning. A few weeks after my rescue, we received a letter from Grace Davies, one of our prayer partners in Warminster.

> We have just received the letter telling of Ray's wonder-ful rescue from the sea. I personally am thrilled to hear this news for a very special reason, which I will tell you.
>
> I was working in the house when I felt a burden to pray for you. At first I brushed it to one side, but the burden grew stronger and stronger. I kept on working until I could resist no longer. I dropped to my knees just where I was in the middle of the lounge and began to intercede for you. I pleaded and cried to the Lord, "Please, please save Ray and Heather from the great danger they are in! I don't know what it is, Lord, but please deliver them!"
>
> I continued to plead with the Lord until the burden lifted. Now I know what it was all about. Isn't our God a great God?

What would have happened if Grace had not been faithful, I can only guess. A heart in constant touch with the Lord through prayer is sensitive to the moving of the Holy Spirit, and I have thanked the Lord many times that Grace Davies kept the lines of communication open between heaven and earth.

Prayer is the most exciting thing a sincere believer can do on this planet. The deeper we go with God, the more we realize how unpredictable His answers are. He is not interested in formulae or rituals. We cannot confine Him to a box and label Him Baptist, Methodist, Anglican, Catholic, Pentecostal or house church.

The Lord's ways are not our ways. He does not work as we work. He is active all the time, in the continuous present. He does not restrict Himself to routines, ruts or programs. He shows up in the most unlikely places, at the most unlikely times and in the most unlikely people. And, we learned, He rarely does things in the same way twice.

At the moment of earnest prayer, we are in touch with the Master Mind, the Creator, the Lord God almighty, who has revealed Himself in human flesh through Jesus the Christ.

During our first missionary journey, Heather and I were sustained time and again by the prayers of our partners back home and by our daily praise and petitions before the Lord. Twice now He had called us to Brazil. And twice we had surrendered to that call. We continued to depend upon the lifeline of prayer for daily direction.

The next phase of our ministry beckoned on the horizon. He had promised to be "a father to the fatherless." Now we awaited the fulfillment of that plan.

6
Through the Fire

Don't be afraid,
for I have ransomed you;
I have called you by name;
you are mine. . . . When you
walk through the fire . . .
the flames will not consume you.

Isaiah 43:1–2, LB

Our return to Brazil felt like a homecoming. We were ready and trained, we thought, to pursue our work with abandoned children. We had been invited to help an elderly lady missionary who was running a small orphanage and we were excited at the prospect. With us were Susan, now eighteen, Andrew, sixteen, and Timothy, five.

Missionary colleagues on furlough had made their Sao Paulo home available to us and, for transportation, friends had loaned us an old kombi, a Brazilian-made Volkswagen mini-van that could seat ten people.

As for a plan of action, we would begin by helping at the orphanage and let the Lord lead us from there. We were His eager missionaries, ready to go where He directed us and obey His marching orders. Prayer would be our main sustenance.

We were not at all prepared, however, for the shattering events that nearly destroyed us, events that seemed orchestrated in the pit of hell.

People are tempted, when sudden disaster strikes or troubles assail, to question why. Heather and I did that. And when faith is shaken to the roots and the enemy tears us apart, we are sometimes left gasping for breath. We experienced that, too. I kept learning that in the throes of our zealous pursuit of God's will, we believers sometimes forget a basic principle: God is sovereign. He is in control of all that happens. He is working behind the scenes and in the scenes to forward His purposes.

When the enemy comes "in like a flood," I was discovering

that God allows him to do so for a reason sometimes known only to Him, that He must occasionally grant the enemy a certain amount of rope in order to accomplish His own overall plan.

Unfortunately, because of the surprise element in most of Satan's attacks, we do not always perceive the hand of God at work. We are overwhelmed by fear, anger, despair or just plain panic, and we become blinded to the presence of our living Lord who has promised never to leave or forsake us.

It is only as we look back on our moments of crisis that we know the Lord was nearer than we had dreamed. And that He was working in that trial for our good and His glory.

Poor Pepper, one of our dogs, was one casualty of Satan's assaults during those early days back in Sao Paulo. I will never forget how pitiful the scraggly gray terrier looked as she lay, mouth open, panting for breath on the vet's examining table. We thought she was suffering from a simple case of distemper and that it would only be a matter of days before she was amusing us with her antics again. But the serious look on the vet's face as he examined her with the aid of a long spatula concerned me.

Finally he issued the verdict: "I believe your dog has rabies. You must get her to the Pasteur Rabies Institute as soon as possible. Whatever you do, don't let any of her saliva get on your skin. If that saliva penetrates into the bloodstream through a scratch or sore, it could be fatal."

Andrew frowned. He had carried his beloved pet on his lap throughout the twenty-minute trip to the veterinarian's office. Pepper's head had rested on his arm. Now as I glanced down at my son's sleeve, I could see a glob of foamy saliva.

"Do you think I'll be all right, Dad?" he asked, clearly worried.

That question haunted me all night. Was Andrew's life in danger? Could a trace of that deadly saliva have entered a crack in his skin? As I thought of the doctor's dire warning, I was almost paralyzed with fear.

Compounding the problem was the fact that this was only the latest in a series of frustrating incidents: I had been taken seriously ill shortly after arriving back in Sao Paulo; then we had been compelled to move three times in five months, after which we had been robbed. And now the dreaded rabies.

The problems generated by this disease were considerable. All the people who had visited our home or come in contact with the dog in the four weeks prior to the diagnosis had to be traced and informed that they must undergo a painful course of anti-rabies injections administered in the abdomen. Not the most pleasant news to deliver to one's friends and neighbors!

And every time I thought of Andrew's question, I could see Pepper's contorted, foaming mouth resting on his arm. I could not put it out of my mind.

After thrashing restlessly most of the night, I got up about five o'clock, feeling sick and utterly exhausted. The powers of darkness seemed determined to rob us of our peace, of our joy in the Lord and of any effective witness we might have for God in Brazil. And we seemed no nearer our goal of ministering to needy children than ever. A question that had been put to us by a recent visitor re-formed in my mind: "What have you done to deserve all this?"

How the enemy rushes in when we consider that question! The devil is called the "accuser of the brethren," but we sometimes forget that he is also God's accuser. His chief objective is to rob God of the glory, praise and honor due Him. If we take our eyes off Jesus, who is holy and just in all His ways, we will soon be hopelessly enmeshed in spiritual darkness and oppression.

That is exactly what happened over the rabies incident. It was the last straw! I could think of nothing but the terrible threat to

Andrew's life and the possibility that the Lord had deserted us.

How subtle Satan is in his attempts to deceive the children of God and rob them of the richness of their inheritance in Christ Jesus! One of his most cunning methods—and yet one that quickly exposes his activity if we are on the alert—is the accusation that "everything is going wrong!" And yet I must confess that those are the words that lived with me during those awful days.

God's Word assures us that "in all things God works for the good of those who love him, who have been called according to his purpose" (Romans 8:28). If, in an off-guard moment, we begin to feel sorry for ourselves, our line of defense against the enemy begins to crumble. And if we indulge in too much self-pity, we fall neatly into his trap.

From the bottom of one of Satan's snares, I looked up and fixed my eyes again on the only One who could save me. As I cried out to the Lord in my desperation that morning, He drew near and answered through His Word:

> Be self-controlled and alert. Your enemy the devil prowls around like a roaring lion looking for someone to devour. Resist him, standing firm in the faith, because you know that your brothers throughout the world are undergoing the same kind of sufferings. And the God of all grace, who called you to his eternal glory in Christ, after you have suffered a little while, will himself restore you and make you strong, firm and steadfast. 1 Peter 5:8–10

I took special note of the phrase *a little while,* drawing some comfort from the implication that suffering does not last forever! With such clear teaching from the Word, it was not difficult to begin praising Him once again as the Lord of all circumstances.

Pepper died that day of rabies. All our recent visitors joined with members of the family at the Pasteur Institute to begin the course of twelve abdominal injections. Thankfully, we all survived the ordeal, and much praise was offered to God that no one contracted the dread disease.

Heather helped me learn an invaluable lesson during those difficult days. She, too, was facing spiritual setbacks. This second missionary journey was exacting a grim toll on her strength and emotions.

I mentioned earlier that I had been taken ill. Exactly one month after our return, I contracted typhoid fever, requiring Heather's nursing care 24 hours a day. She was forced to abandon her visits to the orphanage in Sao Paulo and for several weeks she spent all her time with me. Then, with the onset of pernicious anemia, my condition deteriorated, and Heather fervently sought the Lord in my behalf.

When the doctor told her that only a miracle could save my life, she was able to look him in the eye with perfect confidence and tell him that the Lord had shown her I would not die. In 48 hours, I made a remarkable recovery, and Heather was overjoyed, thanking the Lord for yet another miracle.

On the heels of spiritual victory, however, often comes a spirit of oppression. Taking advantage of Heather's exhaustion in caring for me all those long weeks, and her discouragement over our lack of progress in the ministry, the accuser mounted a vicious attack against her, calling her a failure, a deceiver, a hypocrite and a liar. She was devastated and could not throw off the despair.

One day, at the lowest point of her depression, Heather threatened to take the next flight back to England.

Our daughter Sue suddenly rose to her feet in protest. "Listen, Mum," she said. "We know the Lord has called us here, and that we're in the right place. If you get on a plane and walk right out of the will of the Lord, what will happen to us?''

"Yes, darling," I added, "remember that *all* things, even those things we don't understand, are working together for our good because we love God and have been called by Him."

A glimmer of light sparkled in her eyes. "Well, then." She smiled. "That means that even my doubts, fears and lack of faith must, in some way, be working for our good, doesn't it?"

For a moment I was stunned. It was true. I had no rebuttal for such logic. As I thought it through, I realized that Heather had brought to me a great spiritual secret.

"You're right!" I all but shouted. "Let's praise God together that even those things that seem so negative are actually working for our good."

We joined hands in the center of the room and thanked the Lord that He makes no mistakes in any of our circumstances, but gives us new insight and strength to work through our problems.

Leaving us, Heather went into the bedroom and closed the door. Later, she shared with me the fellowship she had enjoyed with the Lord during those moments.

"I opened my Bible," she told me, "and noticed a loose slip of paper, torn from a calendar. I was surprised to see it because only a few days ago, I had gone through my Bible carefully, taking out all the texts and notes I had been saving because of their special meaning in my life. I smoothed out the paper and read the verse printed there: 'Simon, Simon, Satan has asked to sift you as wheat. But I personally have prayed for you, that your faith will not fail.'

"It was too much!" she confessed. "This gentle word from Jesus to Peter pierced my heart. It was His word to me, too. He loves me so much that He is praying for me personally and is committed to bringing me through this trial. I broke down and wept.''

This was not just a chink of light in a pitch-black tunnel for Heather, but the Light Himself coming into her tunnel with her. We were reminded of the words of Job: ''Surely I spoke of things I did not understand, things too wonderful for me to know. . . . My ears had heard of you but now my eyes have seen you'' (Job 42:3, 5).

Of all the servants of God in the Bible, no one experienced the floods of the enemy's onslaughts as Job did. Satan was given permission by God to test this man's faith to the limit. Robbers stole all his cattle and donkeys; fire destroyed his flocks of sheep; enemy raiders captured all his camels; his servants were murdered; and all his children were killed in a tornado!

As if this were not enough, Satan also received permission to afflict Job's health. He produced terrible, painful sores in God's servant from the top of his head to the soles of his feet. So great was poor Job's anguish—physically, mentally and spiritually— that he cried out: ''Why did I not perish at birth, and die as I came from the womb?''

When a child of God is crushed by some terrible tragedy or overwhelmed by attack, what help can be offered? When a servant of God is numbed by the reality of a great loss and repeats the words of Job, ''What I feared has come upon me,'' how shall we console that person?

Certainly not with the accusations that the devil hurls at him: ''You've gone wrong somewhere along the line!'' Nor by the glib comment of one of Job's would-be comforters: ''Man is born to trouble as surely as the sparks fly upwards!''

The glorious rainbow that broke through the cloud of gloom over Job is his inspired utterance ''When he has tested me, I shall come forth as gold.''

Heather had been tested in the Refiner's fire. Now she shone, gold-bright, as she went about her daily activities.

In the spring of 1978, I moved into the home of Al and Verna Roberts, a missionary couple from Canada, due to return to North America for a five-month leave. Since we needed larger accommodations this was a gift from the Lord, but it meant that we would have to look after two houses for about ten days in order to avoid being robbed. It was decided that Andrew and I would sleep in the Roberts' home until the rest of the family could make the move at the end of the ten days.

The timing of this provision was providential for, as soon as I moved in, I sensed that God wanted to speak to me in a unique way. His presence was so real and so near in that home that it took my breath away.

Every time I picked up the Bible or went into Al and Verna's library, I read something pertaining either to God's will or to man's will. In no way could this have been coincidence, for the teaching was deep and comprehensive, and pointed to a troublesome question I had been asking myself: "Who runs my life, God or me?"

I thought I had answered that question. That I had surrendered my will to the Lord. That Jesus was Lord of my life. That there was nothing I was not willing to do, if He would only make it clear to me. So why this nagging doubt? And why had He not opened up the work of caring for needy children we felt He was preparing for us in Brazil?

God had been strangely silent for months, while my faith had faltered in the stiff wind of adversity. There had been only frustrating delays at every turn, and I was drained physically, exhausted emotionally, and burned out spiritually. Not much to recommend me for an audience with the King of kings. Yet He had made it abundantly clear that this was precisely what He had in mind.

Before going to bed that first night, I opened Watchman Nee's book of meditations and read the entry for April 6: "Sometimes God has to vindicate his own holiness, putting his servants into the fires of suffering. The great test in that hour is their reaction to his governmental hand. When David realized this was God's way, he bowed to it and worshiped the will of God. Should such an occasion arise, could we do this?"

Well, could I? Would I? The questions reverberated in my brain long after I had gone to bed.

The next morning I made porridge for Andrew and saw him off to work at the Evangelical Library, where he had a job with our friends the Barkleys. Then I fed the dogs and cleaned up quickly, looking forward to some undisturbed time with the Lord.

Settling into a comfortable chair, I turned to Ezekiel 2 and read: "You must speak my words to them, whether they listen or fail to listen, for they are rebellious. But you, son of man, listen to what I say to you. Do not rebel like that rebellious house. . . ."

Being unwilling to do the will of God is rebellion. If we detect the slightest unwillingness in our hearts to do what the Lord has asked us to do, we must seek Him with all our hearts for grace and strength to be willing.

I went into the library and picked a volume from a set of nine entitled *The World's Great Sermons*. I asked the Lord to guide my thoughts. What would He have me learn from this book? I opened it and began to read a sermon by John Newton. Again, it was about the will of God.

Although I found some of the language archaic, the sermon was powerful and spoke to my heart, especially the words of Jesus: "I came down from heaven, not to do mine own will, but the will of him that sent me" (John 6:38, KJV). "Not my will, but thine, be done" (Luke 22:42).

Closing the book, I selected another entitled *He Is in Heaven* by Angeline Tucker, the wife of a missionary killed in the strife-torn Congo. The last sermon Brother Tucker had preached in his hometown of Flushing, New York, was on another text quoted in John Newton's sermon: "My meat is to do the will of him that sent me, and to finish his work" (John 4:34, KJV).

After this vivid confrontation with the message the Lord had already placed before me, a battle raged in my mind. I had always known that God's will could mean virtually anything, including physical death. I had been challenged on that score, but I was beginning to see that there was one area I had not abandoned to Him.

What if the Lord asked me to give up my missionary image and go back into teaching? My spirit cringed. Surely He would not bring me all the way to Brazil to teach!

Perhaps, and I dreaded the thought, the Lord might even ask us to return to England without ever fulfilling what we believed He had called us to do.

In my last sermon, preached at Orchard Lane Evangelical Church, Southampton, before setting off on our second missionary assignment to Brazil, I had stated boldly that we desired only to do the Lord's will. My words came back to challenge me now: "If the Lord shows us, even as we are boarding the plane, that He doesn't want us in Brazil, but that it has all been a big test such as Abraham experienced when he was asked to sacrifice Isaac, then we shall stay here in England!"

How easy it had been to utter those words, and how impossible it would be to fulfill them without supernatural grace from God! As it was, we had very nearly been made to eat those words. The flight to Brazil was disrupted by an unexpected strike at London

Airport. We caught a plane to Amsterdam to try to pick up the connecting flight to Brazil, but arrived too late to make the connection.

The Lord then delayed us in Amsterdam for a week, time enough to cause me to consider what I had said at Orchard Lane, and whether or not I really meant it. I was grateful when He showed us that He did not want us back in England so soon, after all, and was giving us a special treat in meeting some wonderful Dutch brothers and sisters in Christ, and spending precious time in the home of Corrie ten Boom.

The questions kept nagging: What if the Lord asked you to go into the British school in Sao Paulo for a time, would you go? Due to a staffing emergency, I had taught there for two weeks while looking after the mission hostel.

But how could I take up a permanent teaching post when all our prayer partners and church friends knew that we were here to work with abandoned and homeless children? Would they feel that we had betrayed their trust? That we were here under false pretenses? Or, and the real truth insinuated itself into my consciousness, would they feel that I had been forced to take a lower position when nothing else opened up for us? I had to admit that our missionary service was a point of pride with me.

I felt sick at heart, for I knew the Lord had touched an area that I would find almost impossible to follow cheerfully. And yet I knew that to turn my back on God's will would be to invite spiritual bankruptcy.

In a book called *They Met at Calvary* by W. E. Sangster, I read the following: "Those who are fully Christian are not 'resigned' to the will of God or acquiescent to it, or just conformed by it, but are abandoned to it. Are you abandoned to the will of God?"

In another chapter I read: "It is so often the consciousness of defeat, of sin, of frustration, that makes us aware of our need of

Him. When our self-assurance is fatally wounded, when we quite honestly don't know what to do, when we drink to the dregs the cup of defeat, when our defenses are down and our pride humbled, God enters through the breach.''

Those words melted my heart! I was convicted. Devastated. Crushed. I knew the Lord had brought me to this point of brokenness to show me that I had no right whatever to lay down any conditions or exceptions to His will for my life. He had brought me back from the jaws of death on at least two occasions and granted me a further period on earth to serve Him. It suddenly seemed not only necessary but possible to abandon myself totally to His will even though it meant the death of my pride—that great stumblingblock of obedience.

I sat down and penned the following thoughts:

> I thought I had something to offer—
> A willing heart,
> My goods to the poor,
> Plans and dreams
> Of exciting things
> For God!
> But then His voice
> Came softly:
> "Draw ye apart awhile
> And meet with Me.
> Come and meet Me
> Face to face.
> Where there are no people
> To sing your praises,
> Or look admiringly,
> To nod their heads
> And speak in glowing terms
> Of your 'faith'!

Come and let Me show you
Your pride!
Your unwilling spirit!
Your deaf ear!
Then . . .
When the ruins of the old house
   are cleared away . . .
I will build another for you.
But . . .
This time it will be Mine!
Unless I, the Lord, build the house,
You labor in vain!''

It is like the riddle "What cannot be useful until it is broken?" The answer is, of course, "An egg." But from experience we know that the answer could just as surely be "A servant of God."

The Scriptures are full of examples of God's servants who had to come to the end of themselves before He could use them— Abraham, Moses, Gideon, Peter, Paul. Jesus Himself told His disciples, "Without Me, you can do nothing."

Until we realize that even with all our natural gifts and talents and resources we are absolutely bankrupt in terms of serving the Lord of all glory, there is not a glimmer of hope that we can be useful to Him.

Sometimes obeying the Lord can be exciting and exhilarating, as when He calls us out of a well-worn rut into pleasant pastures. But sometimes His will can be a great test of love, patience and endurance, as when He takes us through the fires of testing, trial and suffering. In either case, it is *His* will.

Discipline comes to us from God's hand for a purpose. That purpose is to make us productive members of His family. For we are not just servants, but sons of God, called to act like, look like, talk like and be like our Father.

I learned a very valuable lesson that April night. At the time we did not know what the future held for us as a family. We did not know that within a month, I would receive a request to go into the British school in Sao Paulo and that I would spend two-and-a-half fruitful years there. We did not know that, after this period of teaching, we would at last be invited to begin a ministry of founding homes for abandoned children.

But we did learn that true abandonment means to be ready and willing to expect the unexpected. And the unexpected always came . . . right on schedule.

7
Abandoned

If I give all I possess
    to the poor
and surrender my body
    to the flames,
but have not love,
I gain nothing.
Love is patient,
    love is kind.
    1 Corinthians 13:3–4

"Won't you take him?"

Heather and I peered at the stranger on our doorstep. The young African woman held a small bundle in her arms. As she pulled back the faded blanket, we could see that her baby boy was about six weeks of age.

The infant's lips and tongue appeared to be covered with a thick fungus infection. His eyes were shut tightly, and his greasy face was shining as if it had been polished. Rather than having a healthy mahogany sheen, his skin was gray and pasty, and he looked very ill.

With no immediate response from either of us, the mother made another appeal. "Please? I've already tried the orphanage. They say they've got no room for him there and told me to look you up. But if I don't find someplace for him soon, I'll lose my job."

Heather looked down again at the sleeping baby. I knew she was pondering the enormity of caring for yet another child in our crowded quarters, even with Andrew's and Tim's help. (Sue was back in England comforting her grandmother in the loss of her husband.) Just two months before, we had taken in an eight-year-old girl and her six-year-old brother who had been removed from an orphanage by one of our friends due to overcrowding there. Not only that, but we were currently looking after the baby of a missionary couple who were attending a conference. Our responsibilities were multiplying at a rate faster than either of us could keep up with.

A smile replaced the puzzled frown on Heather's face. "Don't you remember the verse of Scripture the Lord gave us yesterday?" she asked me. " 'Anyone who welcomes a child like this, is welcoming Me.' " Turning from the mother's pleadings, she looked into my eyes. "What do you think?"

"Well, my dear, you're the one who will be doing most of the work. A baby will mean more sacrifice, more changes. Do you think you're up to it?"

There was not another moment's hesitation. "If the Lord is bringing this little baby to us, then we must receive him, for it is as if we are receiving Jesus Himself!"

Little John's poor condition proved to be due to neglect and mistreatment by relatives with whom his mother had left him. In addition to the thrush infection and bruises on his body, John's eyes were so swollen that they did not open for the first three days.

Heather worked day and night, trying desperately to feel some affection for this latest addition to our family. Struggling against all kinds of inhibitions and revulsion at his sad state, she finally threw herself on the bed and cried out to the Lord.

"O Lord," she sobbed, "how can I love him when he won't even look at me? Please, Lord, give me Your supernatural love for little John so I can care for him in Your name."

Within a few hours the baby opened his eyes for the first time and gave Heather such an endearing smile that she melted. Tears stung her eyes as she picked John up and cuddled him close, then brought him to show me.

From that moment on, John became our own, bonded by more than flesh and blood. He is now legally our child under both Brazilian and British law. But the relationship was sealed that day in answer to Heather's prayer for a love that sees beyond outward appearances.

While Heather and I were not yet engaged in full-time ministry to the poor and abandoned children we had come to serve, we knew that with the arrival of little John a door was being opened to us by the Lord. I had been teaching in the British school for nearly two years but we were now becoming aware that God was moving us toward the fulfillment of His plan. This awareness was greatly increased about a year after receiving John, when we heard of another little baby who needed a home.

Born two months prematurely, Sara was abandoned by her mother after being placed in the hospital incubator. A British missionary couple, Paul and Rose Jeffery, took Sara a few weeks later when she was strong enough to breathe on her own. Rose, a qualified nurse, was able to care for this tiny baby until a permanent home could be found for her.

When the Jefferys phoned to say they felt the Lord was telling them we should have this baby, we were a bit taken aback. "If that is the case," we countered, "He will just have to show us, too! Bring her 'round, so we can see her, and we'll start praying."

That was on May 30, 1981. The following morning, while having her devotions, Heather opened her book of daily readings, *My Utmost for His Highest* by Oswald Chambers, and read the following extract: " 'And whoso receiveth one such little child in My name, receiveth Me.' God's trust is that He gives me Himself *as a babe*." Our eyes nearly popped out of our heads! We were staggered by such personal words of guidance and such absolute confirmation of God's plan for little Sara. We knew at once that she was a gift of God to us. And a few days later, on June 6, she joined the family.

Because of her premature birth, Sara's digestive system was not sufficiently developed to be able to process cow's milk. The soya substitute with which Heather fed her had a most unpleasant smell and made the routine of nappy-changing a nightmare!

When exposed to the harsh realities of childcare, many people are unable to manage the necessary human empathy, much less love for the unlovely. That is one reason why so many children in the care of local authorities are moved regularly from home to home. Many couples want to help needy children, but discover they do not have the emotional resources to cope with the practical problems.

God's agape love, however, never runs out. His love does not ignore the problems, but finds a way around them or even directly through them. His love enables us to take our eyes off ourselves long enough to focus them on others whose needs are much greater than our own.

Nevertheless, day after day I prayed that the Lord would deliver Heather from the overwhelming stench of those soya-stained nappies. I myself had changed nappies for our four other children, but in Sara's case I found this job so sickening that it became the biggest test of my life when it was necessary for me to do it. Heather took it in her stride, however, demonstrating one of the most remarkable examples of agape love I have ever seen.

The Lord heard my prayers and showed Heather that we should start adding one teaspoon of cow's milk to each bottle of soya formula. A few days later, we added another teaspoon of cow's milk, gradually increasing the ratio each day. Over a period of several weeks, Sara was able to tolerate a whole bottle of regular milk and could then be treated as a normal baby.

With the addition of two babies to the family, Heather sometimes wished that she had Sue's extra pair of hands to help out. Andrew and I both love young children and we helped in as many ways as we could but Andrew, who was now twenty, was about to leave home to join the missionary ship *Doulos*. Young Tim was delighted to have two babies to care for, however, and he lavished brotherly love on them.

Just over a year later, the Lord unwrapped another surprise package for us!

Daniel, our youngest, was born without a left hand, probably because his mother took a drug to abort him. Entering this world in a home for unmarried mothers in Sao Paulo, he was rejected at birth and, because of his handicap, was put up for adoption.

When he was only two weeks old, we were approached by the Brazilian caring agency with whom we worked and asked if we would be willing to take Daniel. Our initial reaction was a negative one. How could we raise a child with a handicap? We had already discussed at length the problems of such children and decided that we were not qualified to care for them.

The hospital continued to plead with us, however, explaining that the baby was taking up space in their nursery needed for other babies.

"At least," they urged, "come see him."

Immediately after we received this request, we took the matter to the Lord and asked Him to give us a sign.

"Look, darling," Heather said to me, "I'll trust your judgment and your decision about this baby. You go to the hospital and see him, then come and tell me how you feel."

The next day I stood at the main entrance to the hospital in Sao Paulo and once more prayed for direction. Tim, who had begged to come with me, stood at my side. Together we entered the vestibule.

Suddenly my gaze was drawn to a poster fixed to a wall ahead of me. It showed an abandoned child standing in the middle of a deserted street. Printed across the poster were the following words in Portuguese: "He who receives a little child like this, in My name, receives Me."

I stood transfixed. These were the same words that God had given us before we received both John and Sara.

Without ever setting my eyes on the child, I had no doubts from that moment that he was being given to us by the Lord Himself. When the nurse held him up for us to see for the first time, his face was bright-red and wrinkled from screaming. There was nothing attractive about him, but I knew he was going to be our new son.

On the way home, Tim and I could not get through the heavy Sao Paulo traffic fast enough. We knew Heather and the other children were waiting to see what our decision had been. As soon as she saw the smile on my face, she knew.

"He's ours, isn't he? While you were gone, the Lord showed me from His Word."

The words from Mark 9:43 had almost leaped off the pages of Heather's Bible as she sat quietly reading during a moment's respite from her work: "It is better to enter life with only one hand, than with two hands to go to hell."

We could not start adoption proceedings until little Daniel had been examined by three doctors—a neurologist, a pediatrician and an orthopedic specialist—to determine if he had any other handicaps.

I shall never forget the moment when the three doctors completed their examinations. Daniel lay screaming on the examining table. As I picked him up and nestled him close, whispering soothing sounds in his ear, such love welled up inside that I knew we had received another gift from God. Even if there were other kinds of physical or mental problems, we would not reject him or turn him away. He was our child, another representative of our beloved Lord.

*   *   *

Having struggled for years with a stale, ritualistic religion, I could recognize the Lord's strategy. He was now regularly providing object lessons in love through these helpless children who came to us. And they in turn received our love and gave it back freely.

One morning, while I was working in the office of our home, the door opened and little John, who was about two years old at the time, toddled in. It was only half past nine and he was not normally allowed to visit me there until coffee break an hour later.

"What are you doing here, John?" I asked, attempting to sound stern.

He clutched my leg, slid down onto his tummy and lay across my feet like a puppy. "I just want to be wif you, Daddy." He smiled an irresistible smile. "I wuv you."

"I love you, too, John." Tears sprang to my eyes, and I cleared my throat. "Now you must be quiet while Daddy works."

I was soon involved with my monthly accounts and, for several minutes, forgot John was there. Suddenly I realized that the soft, warm bundle across my feet had grown very heavy. Looking down, I saw that John was sound asleep! How it reminded me of Corrie ten Boom's quip, often quoted by my father while he was living: "Don't wrestle, just nestle."

Our top priority must always be that intimate love relationship with the Lord that He has enabled us to enjoy by pouring out His Spirit into our hearts. Such love is content to stay close to the Beloved, trusting Him, resting in Him.

When we love someone, we also delight in showering them with tokens of our affection—kisses, hugs, flowers, chocolates, presents of all kinds. The children have often surprised me with some homemade expression of their love—a scribbly picture drawn and colored painstakingly, a handful of daisies picked from our own flower garden. Of such is the Kingdom of heaven.

One night at the children's bedtime, I entered their little room to help tuck them in. Sara, all damp and rosy from her bath, came running to greet me and climbed up on my knee with her favorite storybook.

Throwing her arms around my neck, she began whispering in my ear. "I love you, Daddy," she said, "and when it's your birthday, I'm going to buy you a big box of toffees. And a donkey! A real donkey! And I'm going to ask the Lord to put a rainbow in the sky!"

Sara knows the things I love. And because she loves me, she is willing to go to great lengths to give me my heart's desires. How much more, then, does the Lord delight in giving us good things?

But it made me wonder about our love for Him. How much of my life is spent in trying to delight the Lord by giving Him the desires of His heart? One of His greatest desires is for us to love one another with His kind of perfect, pure agape love. How often was that a priority?

Daniel has taken a leaf out of the Lord's Book already. He is now a dab hand at being a "messenger of love." It all started one day when he said to Heather, "I'm going upstairs to ask Daddy for some sellotape."

"All right," she said. "Give him a kiss for me while you're there."

He knocked on my bedroom-cum-office door and boldly marched in. Stretching up toward me, he pulled my head down to his level and gave me a big kiss on the cheek. "I love you, Daddy," he said, "and that kiss is from me. Now this one is from Mummy!" Pursing his little lips, he gave me another.

As he stood there with a big, broad, cheeky grin on his face, I replied, "Well, that's lovely. Now you can take some kisses back for Mummy with the sellotape.'' With that, I kissed him once on each cheek, once on the nose and again on the lips.

It was no surprise to hear later from Heather that each kiss had been delivered exactly as it had been given, with an extra one added from himself.

What a picture of our role as messengers of love for the King of all kings, who is the King of love. This is not to suggest, of course, that love is merely a matter of kisses. True love is not sloppy or sentimental or contrived. True love seeks to help, encourage and bless others. It is the very life of God put into action, the language of the Kingdom of God.

God is love in its highest form. It is this perfection and purity that God wants to impart to His people through the dynamism of the Holy Spirit. When the world witnesses this kind of love it stops in its tracks and takes notice.

Most of us in the Western world have not been called upon to suffer the hardships, deprivation and persecutions of our brothers and sisters in third-world and atheistic countries. Such eyewitness accounts as *The Hiding Place* by Corrie ten Boom, *Tortured for Christ* by Richard Wurmbrand and *I Love Idi Amin* by Festo Kivengere are far removed from our lives and experience. The high quality of God's kind of love as expressed by these saints has matched up with Scripture, but not with many of our church fellowships!

In Britain, because of our traditions, natural inhibitions and sins of pride and self-love, the flow of God's love has been stifled, if not actually blocked in our churches. The time has surely arrived when we need to cry out to God to grant us the will and the grace to remove these barriers that hinder His love from flowing out to one another and to the lost.

8
On the Rubbish Dump

And if you spend yourselves
   in behalf of the hungry
and satisfy the needs
   of the oppressed,
then your light will rise
   in the darkness,
and your night will become
   like the noonday.
                    Isaiah 58:10

About 45 miles north of Sao Paulo is a small town set like a precious jewel among emeralds. Because of its excellent climate and scenic attractions, Atibaia is a popular tourist resort, frequented by both national and international visitors.

In December 1980, our prayers for ministry were answered at last! We were invited by a Brazilian missionary organization based in Atibaia to help realize their vision for abandoned children: construction of single-unit homes where Christian families could adopt up to ten children.

When the first house was completed, we moved in. Compared to the cramped little apartment in which we had lived for three years, this house at Recanto, seven miles from the town, was a mansion. We looked out over sculptured hills, lush and undulating in the hot Brazilian sun and studded with orange groves, banana plantations and palm trees.

It was an ideal location for a work with children, and we were overwhelmed with the Lord's generosity. We were doubly grateful because we knew this was but another example of His perfect timing and provision. Many times over the previous four years, He had given the promise "Those who wait for me shall never be ashamed" (Isaiah 49:23, LB), but we were staggered by the bounty of His supply when it came.

Waiting is not easy for any of us, but in God's purposes, it is essential in order to test our call, our motives and our abandonment to Him. When these have been purified by the test of time, the Lord will open the door of His appointment. And it will be thrilling!

We soon discovered, however, that there were drawbacks to living in such splendid isolation. One of them was a very practical matter: There was no weekly garbage collection by the local authorities. We had to dispose of all our garbage either by digging a pit and burying it, or by putting it into sacks and transporting it ourselves into the town.

We tried the first method for a week, only to find that a pack of hungry dogs unearthed the buried rubbish during the night and scattered it all over the garden.

I asked our friend Roger, who lived on a nearby *estancia,* where I might leave our sacks of rubbish in Atibaia. He directed me to a market at the entrance to the town, where I should find large metal drums in which to place the sacks. I set off, confident that I had solved a major domestic problem.

Arriving at the marketplace I searched for the drums. Not one could be found. Though I walked the entire length of the market, I could not find a single drum or bin anywhere. Discouraged, I slumped into the driver's seat of our kombi and started the engine. Even though the kombi is large enough to seat ten people, six sacks of smelly garbage more than filled the space inside.

Noticing a scruffy-looking man with a broad grin on his face, I called to him, "Is there a place near here where I can deposit rubbish?"

"Oh, you want the dump!" he exclaimed. "It's that way." With a nod of his head and a flick of his thumb, he indicated the main highway that ran from Sao Paulo to Belo Horizonte. "Just across that road you'll see a narrow track. It leads straight to the rubbish dump."

With renewed hope, I turned the car in that direction. Following the dirt road, which led first to a brick factory, I drove tentatively over the rough terrain behind some bushes until, rounding a bend, the road opened out onto a huge area littered with trash.

There seemed to be three levels to the dump. The lower level was boggy and marshy where a nearby river had overflowed its banks during recent heavy rains. The middle layer had been bulldozed, obviously in an effort to cover mounds of rubbish deposited by lorries from Atibaia and neighboring communities. The top layer, which contained huge piles of soil, was covered with a variety of trash.

As I approached this top level by means of a muddy track, I could see women and children and lots of dogs scavenging through the filth of rotting food, torn wrappings, broken bottles and twisted metal.

Some scantily clad boys no more than ten years of age turned and stared at me when I stopped the kombi about twenty meters from them. As soon as I jumped out and turned toward the rear door to pull out the sacks, they whooped with delight and ran straight for me like savages.

Almost before the door was open, they had grabbed the six sacks and torn them open. Each one plucked some "treasure" out of the decaying rubbish and went scurrying off to show their less adventurous friends who were still sizing up the stranger to their territory.

I climbed back into the driver's seat in disbelief. I could see one boy eating a piece of stale bread he had picked out of the sack. Another was clutching a broken plastic car and still another was holding up to his chest an old T-shirt several sizes too small for him. A fourth boy was looking at me with a shy smile and waving, as if to say, "Please come back!"

And I did go back. But not until I had spent some time in prayer, asking the Lord what He was expecting of me regarding this motley group of very needy people.

*   *   *

As Christmas approached, I felt sure the Lord was directing me to take food parcels to each family who worked among the rubbish. It seemed that they had made a business of rescuing anything of value—newspaper, plastics, firewood, old toys, clocks, radios and a hundred other items that had lost much of their identity. But there was precious little nutritious food to be found. So the whole family joined me in making up neatly decorated packets of rice, biscuits, soup powder, milk and chocolate.

If ever the words of the Lord Jesus "It is more blessed to give than to receive" were true in my own experience, it was on that Christmas Eve when I visited the rubbish dump. There were looks of awe on the faces of the mothers as they received and opened their parcels, and exclamations of *"Graças a Deus!"* which I understood immediately as "Thanks be to God!" As I continued to hand out the packets, I was able to tell them simply that it was, indeed, because of God's love that the gifts were given.

I drove back home, feeling a warm glow in my heart and singing at the top of my voice:

> "He is Lord, He is Lord,
> He is risen from the dead and He is Lord.
> Every knee shall bow, every tongue confess
> That Jesus Christ is Lord!"

In the midst of this private celebration, I heard an unmistakable voice, still and small. *And what about tomorrow?*

"Excuse me, Lord. Did You say something?"

And what about tomorrow? came an echo.

"Tomorrow, Lord? What about tomorrow?"

What will they do tomorrow, and the next day, and the next?

"Lord!" I exclaimed. "What are You saying?"

He then proceeded to show me. As I thought about that question and all the Scriptures and confirmations He had given us over the past six years since our arrival in Brazil, I knew that He was opening the door of His divine appointment. Even more than a home for abandoned children, the Lord wanted me to minister to these outcasts on the rubbish dump! And thus began a ministry that was to teach me more about prayer and its power for life's nitty-gritty than all of my previous Christian experience put together.

As we learn to live in the presence of the Lord, talking to Him and listening to Him, He will show us His plans so that we can pray for the right things. This is what Jesus meant when He said, "And I will do whatever you ask in my name, so that the Son may bring glory to the Father. You may ask me for anything in my name, and I will do it" (John 14:13–14).

In seeking the Lord about the community of poor people living and working on the rubbish dump, He showed me that He wanted His love to be demonstrated to them in two ways: food for the body and then food for the spirit. As a matter of fact, He was very specific. Each time I visited the dump, I was to line up all the children at the door of the kombi and serve each one a cup of milk as he or she repeated a Bible verse.

The day soon came when everything was to be set in motion. The plastic beakers, the milk, the candies (fudge and coconut ice), along with a notebook and pen to record the names of the children, were neatly packed in a large wooden box. These were at my side when I pulled up in front of a group of urchins who were rummaging through a pile of rubbish.

As usual, I got out of the kombi to unload the sacks of domestic trash I had brought from home.

Suddenly I heard a shout in Portuguese: "Look what he's got in here!"

I glanced up toward the front of the vehicle to see a pair of muddy legs sticking out of the window. The rascal had obviously jumped up to see if there was anything of value inside, and decided to help himself to some of the candy in the box.

With a bit of firm discipline, reminiscent of my teaching days, order was soon restored, and the children lined up to receive their milk. The verse they were to repeat was John 14:6: *"Jesus disse: Eu sou o caminho, e a verdade, e a vida"* ("Jesus said, I am the way and the truth and the life").

The children repeated the words hesitantly, some with giggles, some with puzzled expressions on their faces. But as they spoke the life-giving words of Jesus, I was interceding for them that God would pour out His love and blessings and anoint the words so they would take root in each childish heart and bear eternal fruit for His glory.

Almost as soon as my work with the needy children on the rubbish dump had commenced, the enemy attempted to destroy it. He used all kinds of tactics, including direct opposition from his own agents, a group of hardened spirit-worshipers who lived there. Sometimes, after I arrived, these people would try to persuade the older boys and girls to stay away from the kombi. Judging by the furtive looks I received from these children while they continued working in the rubbish, I suspected they were being threatened or intimidated.

There were other, more subtle snags in the early days of that work. Some of the older children often used my visits as occasions to demonstrate their anger and frustration against a society in which they had become outcasts. They would shout me down and mimic my mannerisms, developing an infinite variety of techniques designed to harass. There was much muttering and grumbling about their hard life. And occasionally they even tried to damage the kombi as it sat parked near the dump. It was their way of protesting a bleak and hopeless future, which for many of the girls seemed to be prostitution and, for the boys, a life of crime or alcoholism.

But perhaps the most difficult hurdle of all was my own discouragement. Knowing that I would be coming here indefinitely, I was filled with revulsion by the sights and smells. Nothing in my rather reserved upbringing had prepared me for the muck, the filth, the stench that literally nauseated me.

Many times in those first few weeks, I returned home feeling overwhelmed. I knew God had called me to the dump, but I had not expected it to be quite so hard. And I had thought that the people would receive me with gratitude, not this overt, sometimes violent rejection.

In retrospect, I suppose I was guilty once more of pride. Being by nature a workaholic, I brought all my best energies to bear on this mission to which the Lord had called me, and in the process, I think His plan became mine.

This sin of pride seems to emerge especially in those of us who have positions of leadership or prominence in God's service. It is so sneaky, creeping in under the carpet, just like the ants, cockroaches, poisonous spiders and scorpions common to Brazil. The answer, I have discovered, is to confess and renounce it as soon as the Holy Spirit brings it to light.

We think we are abandoned to God when we accept His call, and can minister without being tainted by it. Then we say, "Search me, O God, test me. See if there is any offensive way in me." And He exposes this cunning, egotistic tendency of ours to take some of the credit for what He alone has done. How important it is that we watch and pray against pride so that the Lord is not robbed of any of His glory, and so His perfect plans are not hindered by our intervention!

Some of us also fall into the error of praising God's servants for what is so obviously His work. This is a great snare of the enemy, not only for the servant who may be mightily tempted to pride, but also for the onlookers who are doing the devil's work of robbing God of the glory He deserves.

No one would think of applauding a postman, a printer or a bookseller for some great masterpiece of literature that falls into our hands, though each may have been responsible in some way for its safe arrival. The Author of life and of our salvation is the only One worthy of glory and praise for what He is doing in these days of His outpoured Spirit.

One day when I was driving along the dirt road leading from our home to the rubbish dump, black clouds gathered suddenly, as they often do in the hot season. Great masses of darkness billowed against a background of sunlit white clouds.

That's it! I thought. *I'm not meant to go today. It's going to pour down!* Secretly in my heart, I knew I should be there, rain or shine. But I had grown so discouraged by the outrageous behavior of some of the teenagers that any excuse not to go would do.

As I turned the last bend in the road and saw the high mound of red earth that marked the dump site, my eyes were drawn upward. There in the sky, spanning the whole area of the slum community, was a rainbow. I had never seen one so big, so close, so vivid.

My whole being was overshadowed by the presence of the Lord, and my heart swelled in praise. "Yes, Lord," I whispered. "You are here. You are the Lord of the rainbow, and You are the Lord of this rubbish dump."

From that moment I always referred to the dump as *Arco Iris,* which is the Portuguese word for "rainbow."

To most people the rainbow is a sign of hope, a promise of better things to come. To the Christian, however, the rainbow has even greater significance. God's throne is surrounded by a rainbow (Revelation 4:3). It is not just a reminder of God's promise that He will never again flood the whole earth, but a sign that He is alive, active and present with us now in our circumstances.

Suddenly all the obstacles and difficulties associated with this mission assumed their proper perspective, including my own role. As the tears came to my eyes on that morning, I drew off to the side of the road and thanked the Lord for revealing Himself to me in that moment of discouragement. I remembered that when He called me to go to the needy folk on the dump, He had not promised it would be easy, but that He would go with me.

Shortly after that experience, I had a dream that completely transformed my attitude toward the work at Arco Iris. In the dream I was visiting a needy family with many children. Hiding behind all the others was one little boy who caught my eye.

Catching a glimpse of his face, I was moved by the sadness I saw there. His eyes were pools of eternal tears. I knew I could not leave until I had spoken to this child.

At first he would not meet my gaze, but eventually he had no choice, for I stood before him and waited. At last he looked up.

"Jesus Christ is alive *today!*" I told him.

Immediately hope and life returned to those haunting eyes and then I woke up.

The dream had been so vivid I had no doubt it was from the Lord. When I prayed, He revealed its meaning.

This child represents the millions of children throughout the ages who have been without hope, He said. *The poor, the oppressed, the sick, the homeless, the lonely, the rejected, the abandoned of this world—all those who have never heard of Jesus.*

Many times thereafter, when I looked into the grubby faces of the children who appeared at the door of the kombi to receive their cup of milk, I saw those sad eyes and remembered the dream and its message. And the appalling circumstances of their lives faded as I saw them through the eyes of the Lord.

One morning when I arrived to feed the children, an older woman appeared with her young grandchild of about two. Down the side of the little girl's bare body and on both legs were huge blisters.

"What happened to her?" I asked.

"She pulled the cooking pot off the fire early this morning, and the boiling water spilled on her."

"Then you must get her to the hospital," I said. "It's urgent that she receive care for her burns. Come, I'll take you."

When we arrived at the hospital, the child was admitted at once under the free treatment program for destitute patients. As I helped the grandmother complete the admission documents, I thought to myself, *What a humiliating experience to have to write "Rubbish Dump" as one's place of residence!*

And yet how many of the sophisticated, educated and affluent members of our Western society reside in an environment of moral filth and decadence no less abominable than the rubbish dump of Sao Paulo? It is not necessary to go to Arco Iris to find people raking through the muck of our so-called modern "civilization." Thousands of the spiritually impoverished are scavenging through the sordid mess of the polluted morals of our day.

As I prayed for those children and their caretakers by name each day, the Lord created within me a greater desire to see them set free from their misery.

Eventually, in May 1982, the opportunity came to extend the work.

In conversation with some of the mothers one day, the Lord planted a seed in my mind that would later germinate to immense proportions. As I looked at each of those poor women, I thought of their plight. Many of them had been thrown out of their homes by abusive husbands who no longer loved them or wanted them. Others were single mothers whose own parents had disowned them when the pregnancy became obvious. Still others had no other existence outside the rubbish dump. But the fact remained that they were mothers. And most of them loved their children and did the best they could for them.

With Mother's Day approaching, the idea grew. It was to help the children express appreciation to their mothers for their love and care. Heather helped make attractive cards for each mother, along with individually wrapped bouquets of fresh red roses.

On the first Saturday of the month, on my usual visit to the dump, I carried along some colorful invitations to attend a special Mother's Day service the following day. I knew that most of the women would not be able to read the wording, but I scored the day and hour in thick lettering and encouraged the children to be there at 3 o'clock in the afternoon, saying, "There will be a surprise for all your mothers and substitute mothers. So don't be late!"

The following day dawned dull and overcast. By lunchtime it appeared as if the heavens were going to pour down sheets of rain rather than blessings on our service. At Recanto, Heather and our children gathered to pray, pleading with the Lord to hold back the rain and give us a good time in His name.

By 2:30, all the cards, roses and flannelgraph materials were packed in the kombi, along with Heather and our family. Everyone was a bit tense, wondering if any mothers or children would be at the rubbish dump on a Sunday afternoon.

We need not have doubted, for when, just before three o'clock, we veered off the main road onto the last bumpy track toward the dump, we could see in the distance quite a crowd gathered to greet us.

We drove up and piled out of the kombi with a fresh burst of enthusiasm, quietly praising God for the turnout.

Though nearly all the mothers and children were dressed in the same tattered clothing they wore during the week, evidence here and there—a combed head, a scrubbed face—showed that some had made a special effort for the occasion. Large round eyes shone with excitement. And, in spite of the low-hanging clouds threatening rain, we felt an air of anticipation.

When I hung the flannelgraph board on the side of the kombi, the group edged forward and formed an arc around us, anxious to see what would happen next.

I welcomed them all, then placed the figure of a mother and child on the board.

"Mothers are a precious gift," I began. "They feed us . . . clothe us . . . cook for us . . . care for us . . . but, above all . . . love us."

There was not a sound as I added pictures of food, clothing, blankets, soap, a cuddly toy and a large red heart at the top.

As I told the story of Jesus blessing the children, I became aware that a hush had descended over the gathering. These mothers and children were identifying themselves in a special way with the story. So obviously in need of love and care themselves, they were being drawn irresistibly to the One who could love them and care for them like no other.

Concluding the story, I placed the last picture in the center of the flannelgraph board. It depicted Jesus with outstretched arms, children of all races in the foreground, leaning on His knee, looking up into His kind face.

"Let us pray that we may come to know the love of Jesus just as these people in the story knew Him."

For the first time we prayed together, and there was a breath-lessness in the very air. The children and their mothers listened as if half-expecting to hear a voice from heaven.

Then I spoke to the children, reminding them of the significance of this day for their mothers, the ones who cared for them. I took out one of the beautiful red roses, garnished with greens and wrapped in silver foil, explaining that this was a symbol of our love for our mothers. I asked each child to step forward and take one of the roses and a greeting card to present to his or her mother with a kiss as a token of love and gratitude.

One by one they came forward, some shuffling timidly, others marching boldly. Little Mariane, her shining eyes brimming with love, took a rose from Heather's hand and a card from mine. Then, carrying her treasures as if they were the most valuable in the world, she placed them in her mother's extended hand and stretched up to kiss both her tear-stained cheeks.

Eight-year-old Clarisa, her black hair matted, moved shyly to the front. She ducked her head as she accepted the gifts, then returned to her mother, Dona Teresa, who was hanging back on the fringe of the crowd, balancing her youngest on one hip.

Bold Antonio stepped forward—a tough twelve-year-old who lived with his grandmother. With an ear-splitting grin, he snatched the delicate rose from Heather's hand, then stopped, transfixed. He stared at it, unable to tear his gaze away, as if beholding a thing of beauty for the first time in his life. Slowly he turned and walked reverently to his grandmother's side, his eyes still on the velvet petals, his face a study in awe and wonder.

And so they came—Maria das Graças, the happy-go-lucky chatterbox; little Roberto with his large, hungry eyes, clutching the hand of José, his tall, serious-faced brother. All presented their gifts, giving their mothers hugs and kisses as their own personal offerings of gratitude and love.

I glanced around, knowing that behind each little tableau was a heartbreaking story. And I remembered the verses of Scripture the Lord had given me for the mothers and children on this special day: "This is what the Lord says—he who created you . . . : 'Fear not, for I have redeemed you; I have called you by name; you are mine' " (Isaiah 43:1).

God was there with us. Whole families stood with arms clasped about each other as if they wanted the moment to last forever. And in a way, it did. For this was the first of many such occasions. Every Sunday afternoon thereafter, we met on the dump to sing songs of worship, pray together and hear an illustrated message from the Word.

Arco Iris was no longer merely a rubbish heap for the discards of society. On that day we had witnessed the real beginning of hope. On that day we had stood on holy ground.

9
Sentence of Death

Indeed, in our hearts we felt
the sentence of death.
But this happened that we might
not rely on ourselves but on God.

2 Corinthians 1:9

Arriving at the rubbish dump a few weeks after we began the Sunday services, I found the place deserted. Not a soul was to be seen working in the piles of rubbish and an eerie silence shrouded the whole area.

That's strange, I thought. *Where is everybody?*

I sounded the kombi's horn with a few short blasts, but nobody appeared. Dropping into the driver's seat, I rested my arms on the steering wheel and looked about. Except for the absence of people, the scene was much the same as on previous visits.

But there was an aura of evil that hovered like a malevolent spirit. As I drove away slowly, I had no doubt that in invading enemy territory, we had challenged the forces of darkness. And it was equally clear that they had no intention of allowing the Word of God to be proclaimed on the dump without a fight.

Long before coming to Sao Paulo, Heather and I had studied the culture and religious beliefs of the people in this part of the world and knew something of the dark battle we were exposing ourselves to.

Spiritism is widely practiced in South America, with three of the four million adherents alone living in Brazil. Often described as the cult of antiquity, spiritism is the oldest religious cult extant today. In *Kingdom of the Cults* Walter Martin defines spiritism as "the masquerade of demonic forces, who pretend to be departed spirits with the intent of deceiving, through the power of Satan, those foolish enough to believe the testimony of demons in preference to the authority of the Word of God." It is the classic contest between good and evil—God's power versus the power of darkness. It has been present in the world since Satan introduced it to Adam and Eve in the Garden of Eden.

God's Word leaves no room for question about such beliefs:

> Let no one be found among you . . . who practices divination or sorcery, interprets omens, engages in witchcraft, or casts spells, or who is a medium or spiritist or who consults the dead. Anyone who does these things is *detestable to the Lord.*   Deuteronomy 18:10–12

Why mankind clings to this propensity when it is expressly forbidden, I cannot fathom, except to say that it springs from the rebellion born in the Fall. Apparently, people will indulge in whatever it takes to try to enter the spirit world—witchcraft, divination, enchantments—all of which I was to glimpse first-hand in the weeks to come.

Many people dismiss spiritism, unfortunately, as harmless superstition or merely the ignorance of uncivilized peoples. An even more frightening development to me is the popularization of its claims by some celebrities whose books and lectures on the topic have brought a groundswell of interest among thousands seeking some kind of spiritual reality.

But God's attitude toward those who practice these forbidden arts is clear and unequivocal. The Old Testament clearly outlines the penalty for sorcery: death (Exodus 22:18). And for those consorting with "familiar spirits" and "wizards" (male witches): the curse of God (Leviticus 19:31).

Spiritism is a deadly business, and if I had not been convinced before, my skirmish with the sea goddess off the coast of Suarao had made me a true believer in the reality of demonic powers. As the Living Bible renders Ephesians 6:12,

> We are not fighting against people made of flesh and blood, but against persons without bodies—the evil rulers of the unseen world, those mighty satanic beings and great evil princes of darkness who rule this world; and against huge numbers of wicked spirits in the spirit world.

My retreat that day at the dump was not made out of fear, but out of a healthy respect for the opposition! And I returned home determined to seek the Lord's wisdom about what to do. If the people were being warned to keep away from me, as seemed evident, then how could I regain their trust in order to present the message of truth that could release them from their bondage?

As I turned to the Word, the Lord pointed me to some wonderfully reassuring promises and the following morning Heather came to me with additional confirmation. ''The Lord has given me this verse for you—Matthew 16:18. The gates of hell will not overcome you.'' A few minutes later, when I picked up a prayer letter from *Portas Abertas* (Open Doors), and read the same text printed in Portuguese on the front page, I knew the Lord was directing me to go back to the dump immediately.

Armed with Scripture promises, I returned to Arco Iris and was greatly encouraged to see all the people there, working in the rubbish. While not all the children came for their milk, many did. As the Word of God was repeated to each child in turn, its truth sank home to bless my own heart: ''The Lord is my strength and my shield; my heart trusts in him'' (Psalm 28:7).

A few months later one of the young mothers, Dona Cinira, came running up to the kombi as soon as I pulled in.

"Please Pastor," she began breathlessly, "I don't know if my husband is alive or dead! This morning he was stabbed while quarreling with another man over something they found in the rubbish. An ambulance came and took him to the hospital, but he was cut bad."

When a neighbor signaled that she would look after the children, I motioned to Dona Cinira to get in beside me and roared away in the direction of the local hospital. I knew José well. He was one of the few fathers who had shown a friendly interest in me and the work I was trying to do. He and his wife and their five children, ranging in age from two to thirteen, lived in a makeshift shack at the entrance to the rubbish dump. Although I knew José had a serious problem with the cheap, homemade alcoholic drink with which many of the Brazilian poor drown their sorrows, he was at least a hard-working and loving father to his children.

What many do not realize is that spiritism has many faces. While demon spirits may gain access to a person through the practice of "magic arts"—such as the use of incantations or magical words, wearing an article of clothing or jewelry invested with some kind of magical power, or casting spells or curses—other spirits enter a person through the medium of a mind-altering drug, which renders them susceptible to suggestion by the evil power. Though it was not clear whether or not José was possessed by some demon entity, it was clear that his life was in danger, for the hidden powers of darkness, under the supreme command of the devil himself, are out to "rob, kill and destroy."

Upon arriving at the hospital, Dona Cinira and I rushed to inquire about her husband. Learning that he was already in the operating theatre in critical condition, we returned to the dump to pray with the children that their father would be spared. We cried to the Lord, appealing to His mercy and love. In that moment I sensed in my heart that the Lord had heard our prayer and would give José not only physical healing, but eternal life as well.

José's amazing recovery from his serious wounds had a profound effect on him. He knew he was alive for one reason only: God had seen fit to release him from the death sentence. Visiting him in the hospital often, I was able to pray with him and read the Word of God. That sharp, penetrating sword of the Spirit hacked away at all the defenses of his heart. And on a Sunday afternoon not too many months later, we rejoiced to see José's victory over sin when he made his decision to follow the Lord Jesus.

As the Lord's presence and power began to be manifested in specific answers to prayer, we noticed that more and more people were attending the Sunday meetings. Some were drawn initially by the food and occasional items of clothing that we were able to distribute, but many came because of spiritual hunger. And some came as Satan's emissaries, desiring to thwart the purposes of God at Arco Iris.

One Sunday one of the mothers brought with her an evil-looking woman whose eyes were clouded in darkness and whose form was hunched like that of a witch. I discerned immediately an oppressive presence, claimed the power of the blood of the Lamb over the meeting and spent more time than usual exalting the Lord in songs and prayers of praise.

On the following Saturday, the mother asked how I was feeling. When I assured her that I felt fine and that, in fact, we had sensed the presence of God in our home in a special way during the week, she relaxed and looked greatly relieved.

The old woman had almost certainly been an active spiritist who had tried to put a curse on me, as many try to do with evangelical Christians, especially missionaries. But the Word of God quells any fear: "Like a fluttering sparrow or a darting swallow, an undeserved curse does not come to rest'' (Proverbs 26:2).

Though I came to no harm, that incident did alert us to the great need for special prayer covering our visits to Arco Iris. We asked our prayer partners to pray, if possible, during the actual times of the visits. And I made a practice of stopping along the lane leading to the dump to pray for the Lord's protection and blessing before ministering to the needy folk there. At home, Heather gathered the children, and the whole family covered me in prayer while I was on the dump.

The strongholds of the enemy must fall when God's people unite in intercession to bring His will to pass on earth. Prayer releases all the resources of heaven, and gives us access to the hosts of God who will fight beside us.

But the evil old woman's presence was an active reminder of the darkness we must attempt to penetrate with the Light of life.

Now, witches do not always come garbed in black, with a humped back and a wart on the nose! The Bible tells us that evil often comes disguised as an ''angel of light.'' In fact, modern-day witchcraft can be very attractive. Horoscopes, ouija boards and tarot cards to foretell the future, for example, are designed as much to entertain as to delve into the dark mysteries of the spirit world. But for all their ''innocence,'' these pursuits are con-demned by God and should be completely avoided.

Just listen to what God has to say about those who consult horoscopes:

> Let your astrologers come forward, those stargazers who make predictions month by month, let them save you from what is coming upon you. Surely they are like stubble; the fire will burn them up. They cannot even save themselves.
>
> Isaiah 47:13–14

There is yet another form of witchcraft that is often overlooked. ''Rebellion is like the sin of divination [witchcraft], and arrogance like the evil of idolatry'' (1 Samuel 15:23).

Disobedience, rebellion and pride—the besetting sins of the human race—are found not only in the remote reaches of Africa and South America, but in elegant drawing rooms, in corporate boardrooms and in the offices of world government! Whatever form it takes, witchcraft is simply the audacity of people to pit their feeble power against the power of our great God.

One mother came to the services for several months looking sad, as though oppressed by a spirit of gloom, until I preached on Revelation 21:8:

> The cowardly, the unbelieving, the vile, the murderers, the sexually immoral, those who practice magic arts, the idolaters and all liars—their place will be in the fiery lake of burning sulphur. This is the second death.

As I spoke about each category mentioned in this list, I could see that the Lord was working deeply in many lives. The Holy Spirit was convicting their hearts about their need for a Savior who could deliver them from the terrible danger they were in.

Many gave their lives to the Lord that afternoon, but this particular mother was wonderfully delivered from the bondage of fear, depression and hopelessness in which the enemy had held her captive for many years. She told me that she had great concern for her husband who was a *feiticeiro,* a practicer of magic arts.

We sought special prayer for this man and he did eventually come to one of the Sunday meetings, but without committing his life to God. Yet he had been exposed to the Word. We continued to pray for him, leaving the results in the Lord's hands.

Meanwhile we saw so clearly, and stressed over and over again, that a mother and her children who have been born into the Kingdom of God must stand firm against the powers of darkness operating within their own home. They do so only by "the grace of God, by the word of their testimony and by the blood of the Lamb."

Fighting the enemy on his turf is not pleasant. In fact, any Christian connected with Arco Iris had to resist the spirit of fear many times. Paul said,

> Indeed, in our hearts we felt the sentence of death. But this happened that we might not rely on ourselves but on God, who raises the dead. He has delivered us from such a deadly peril, and he will deliver us. On him we have set our hope that he will continue to deliver us.   2 Corinthians 1:9–10

We lived in the strength of that promise.

One night in late winter, I had a vivid dream in which I was shown the importance of allowing the Lord to remain in control of His work, and not to hinder it with my own ideas or the methods of the world.

In the dream I was admiring some beautiful pieces of precious stone when I spotted a fragment of pottery, obviously part of a broken vase. The workmanship was so exquisite that it took my breath away.

Looking up, I saw that a poor African boy was holding the piece of pottery.

"Where did you get this?" I asked.

"From my house."

"Who made it?"

"My father," he said proudly.

"And how much would such a vase cost?"

At this, the boy laughed and shook his head, as if to say, "What a silly question! Why, it is priceless!"

Then I woke up. As I did so, in my mind I suddenly saw a picture of a large, whole vase with the same delicate tracery as the piece that the little boy had been holding. It was the most beautiful thing I had ever seen. The colors, the symmetry and the ornamentation defied description. But on closer inspection, I saw that the vase was made of common clay.

Lying there in bed, I knew the Lord was showing me the vase for a purpose. "But, Lord, it is so delicate and could break so easily! It would take only a careless moment or the wrong pair of hands to render it useless. How can we protect it?"

There is only one way to protect My workmanship, the Lord replied. *Lift it high, out of the reach of men's hands. By lifting it up in prayer and praise, it stays in My control, where no one can harm it.*

Not by human might, nor human strength, nor human ingenuity, nor human methodology, but only by lifting God's work, His plans, His will up to Him and praising Him for what He is doing and what He is going to do. Then we must be obedient to do the thing He gives us as part of the whole plan.

I had completed my basic training at Arco Iris. Now I would soon be ready for hand-to-hand combat with the enemy.

10
Like a Mighty Warrior

The Lord is with me
like a mighty warrior;
so my persecutors will stumble
and not prevail.
They will fail and be
thoroughly disgraced.
Jeremiah 20:11

The enemy had declared war on Arco Iris and there was no doubt in my mind what my role was to be. Any child of God who responds to the call to take up arms against the spiritual powers of darkness is assured support by our Supreme Commander: "The Lord is with me like a mighty warrior."

I shall never forget the day the Lord anointed that word to my heart after several weeks of severe testing at the hands of a group of ruffians. A gang of teenage boys had attempted to sabotage the Sunday services with disruptive behavior—mockery during the singing, interfering with the flannelgraph board during the talks and damaging parts of the kombi when my back was turned.

To further confuse and distract, a pack of about twenty dogs had appeared and stationed themselves in the midst of the group, pushing their wet noses into the faces of the children and sniffing their hands. With such competition, the flannelgraph lesson did not stand much of a chance.

Then I remembered that people were praying—our prayer partners in England and around the world, and Heather and the children at home. In spite of all the turmoil around me, I was at peace and continued on with the lesson. When the time came for the message from God's Word, both dogs and children sat quietly, and the Lord's presence descended upon us.

That afternoon two mothers and several children surrendered their lives to Christ and Jeremiah 20:11 became living reality. The knowledge and certainty that I was doing the will of God with Jesus beside me, in front of me, behind me and inside me was quite sufficient to give me the courage I needed to do the impossible.

The evil at Arco Iris, as overwhelmingly oppressive as it was at times, was only a microcosm of the evil in the world. The battlefield is all around us—in urban centers of culture, in university classrooms, and even in the cushioned pews of our churches. It is as near as our own minds and hearts! Wherever Satan can delude and deceive, he and his demon hordes plot their strategy. He is the "prince of this world" (John 12:31), the "ruler of the kingdom of the air, the spirit who is now at work in those who are disobedient" (Ephesians 2:2).

Since the battlefield may be anywhere at any time, to fail to be filled with the Spirit of God and equipped with His armor is foolishness. No soldier goes into the battle without his weapons. And the Christian warrior is no different. Through God's Word each of us has been issued complete gear for defending himself and for mounting an offensive attack when necessary. Here is the crucial Scripture:

> Be strong in the Lord and in his mighty power. Put on the full armor of God so that you can take your stand against the devil's schemes . . . so that when the day of evil comes, you may be able to stand your ground, and after you have done everything, to stand. Stand firm then, with the *belt of truth* buckled around your waist, with the *breastplate of righteousness* in place, and with your feet fitted with the readiness that comes from *the gospel of peace*. In addition to all this, take up the *shield of faith*, with which you can extinguish all the flaming arrows of the evil one. Take the *helmet of salvation* and the *sword of the Spirit*, which is the word of God. And pray in the Spirit on all occasions with all kinds of prayers and requests.
>
> Ephesians 6:10–11, 13–18

As the Lord's appointed second-in-command at Arco Iris, not only did I need to be fully equipped at all times, but I needed to train the footsoldiers who would be engaged in spiritual warfare there. The children and mothers needed to know all that the Lord had put at their disposal for their protection and survival. I taught them the technique I use.

Early each morning, during my prayer time, I "put on" the following six articles of equipment mentioned above in preparation for the day's battles:

1. *The helmet of salvation* reminds us that we have a Savior and Deliverer whose shed blood has not only cleansed us from all sin, but has also guaranteed us victory over the enemy. Reaffirming this fact daily gives us confidence and faith, and speaking the words aloud lets the enemy know *we* know where we stand.

One of the devil's favorite tactics is to confuse and condemn. If he can lay a guilt trip on us, over some real or imagined sin, if he can make us question our salvation or doubt our forgiveness, he has won a major battle.

Such a thought lodging in my mind is like a time bomb. I defuse it with these words of Jesus:

> "I give them eternal life, and they shall never perish; no one can snatch them out of my hand. My Father, who has given them to me, is greater than all; no one can snatch them out of my Father's hand. I and the Father are one."
>
> John 10:28–30

Our salvation does not depend upon anything we do; it rests in what He has already done!

2. The *breastplate of righteousness* protects the vital area of the heart. In Roman times the breastplate was constructed of bronze backed with hide. Our breastplate is constructed not of

our righteousness, which is as filthy rags (Isaiah 64:6), but His righteousness: "God made him who had no sin to be sin for us, so that in him we might become the righteousness of God" (2 Corinthians 5:21).

When we confessed and repented of our sins, Jesus gave us His spotless robe of righteousness. Satan's accusations of "dirty" thinking and living will fall on deaf ears if we remember that we are acceptable to God through His righteousness (Jeremiah 23:6).

3. The *belt of truth* holds everything together. The Roman girdle, six to eight inches wide, was designed to span the waist. This belt was vital because it secured all the other pieces of the armor.

Truth stabilizes. We had better not go into battle stained with disobedience, deceit or hypocrisy. As we put on the belt of truth, we check ourselves to see if we have put things right with colleagues, neighbors or loved ones we have offended. This is the place each day when I am reminded that I need a fresh filling of the Holy Spirit for, as the Spirit of truth, He can keep me honest in all my dealings. Only He can reveal to me the reality and beauty of Jesus, my Commander, who called Himself the way and the truth and the life (John 14:6).

4. I put on the *shoes of the gospel of peace.*

Peace is the inheritance of every believer. That is why we do not need to give way to the twin foes of fear and anxiety. Many, many times throughout Scripture, the Lord instructs, "Do not be afraid." Since the verb is in the imperative, this is not a suggestion, but the direct command of our divine Commander. He knows that fear is one of the enemy's best offensive weapons, for fear does not originate with the Lord: "God hath not given us the spirit of fear; but of power, and of love, and of a sound mind" (2 Timothy 1:7, KJV).

We drive out fear, worry and stress with the peace of mind

promised every child of God. We need to learn to depend upon God's promises in order to maintain our sure footing in the heat of battle.

When under attack I claim the peace God offers in Philippians 4: "Do not be anxious about anything, but in everything, by prayer and petition, with thanksgiving, present your requests to God. And the peace of God, which transcends all understanding, will guard your hearts and your minds in Christ Jesus" (vv. 6–7).

As we lace up our combat boots, we are reminded that, throughout the day, our feet will take us to places of opportunity to speak and live for Jesus Christ. These are mapped out for us each day. We must be sensitive to the fact that every person in our life has been placed there by the Master Strategist for His own purposes. There are no coincidences with Him. As we put on these shoes symbolically, we receive by faith His divine appointments for the day. Life takes on an aura of excitement as we look for them and ask the Lord to fulfill His purposes through us.

5. The *shield of faith* is another vital weapon.

A Roman soldier's long shield was about two feet wide. He used it to ward off individual blows of the enemy and also arrows from enemy archers.

Satan launches his missiles against us, but the shield of faith acts as a barrier. The enemy's artillery falls harmlessly to the ground and fizzles out when meeting this kind of resistance.

It is interesting that Paul, when giving his instructions to the Ephesian believers, says, "Take up the shield of faith, with which you can extinguish *all* the flaming arrows of the evil one." We can count on complete protection against Satan's offensive weapons if we exercise our faith. Not one dart will penetrate our defenses.

As we take up this shield we should be praying: "Lord, You are my shield against the assaults of the enemy. You are my rock, my fortress and my deliverer; You are my rock in whom I take refuge'' (see Psalm 18:2).

Since Jesus is the same yesterday, today and forever, His authority, power, anointing, promises and commission are also the same for those who seek to follow Him and do His will. He is looking for soldiers whose faith demonstrates that we will abandon ourselves to Him alone and not depend on our own makeshift attempts to protect ourselves. This kind of faith is born out of time spent in communion with Him, whereby we hear Him speak to our hearts. Only the words of the living Christ create faith of the quality that moves mountains and pulls down enemy strongholds.

6. The last piece of armor, the *sword of the Spirit,* God's Word, is the only offensive weapon in Paul's listing of spiritual armor. We have discussed the other offensive weapon—prayer— earlier. A quick word about that in a moment.

In ancient times the sword was the ''smart bomb'' of warfare. The long blade was serrated on both edges and pointed on the end. It could thrust and penetrate from any position the Roman soldier might choose, thus catching his opponent off-guard while maintaining his own balance.

''The word of God is living and active. Sharper than any double-edged sword, it penetrates even to dividing soul and spirit, joints and marrow'' (Hebrews 4:12). When the Christian soldier wields this weapon by quoting Scripture that targets the crisis at hand, Satan flees.

Here is an example of wielding the sword of the Spirit.

One Sunday while preparing to go to Arco Iris, a strange lethargy and tiredness came over me. I went into the bedroom to rest and pray, but an hour later I felt so weak and ill-equipped to face the demands of the children and their parents that I told

Heather I was going to cancel the visit. She suggested we see what the Lord had to say.

After praying with me for a few minutes, she left me alone again. As she closed the door, I reached for my Bible. "Lord, You know I want to go and give these dear people Your words of hope and love," I whispered, "but how can I stand before them when I feel as weak as a kitten?" I opened the Bible at random to Revelation 3 and started reading: "These are the words of him who is holy and true, who holds the key of David. What he opens, no one can shut; and what he shuts, no one can open. I know your deeds. See, I have placed before you an open door that no one can shut. *I know that you have little strength. . . .*" (vv. 7–8)

At that moment, tears came to my eyes. I realized that, despite my great weakness, I was linked to the Power Source of all eternity. I knew that I could now stand on my feet and proclaim those living words to the enemy of my soul who had to flee before them. And flee he did.

As I set off for the rubbish dump filled with excitement and fresh hope, I cried to the Lord to send His Holy Spirit upon us all so that everyone gathered at the dump might receive a similar personal word from Him. I renounced my weakness and opened myself to the Lord's strength. It was a precious experience to see how He moved among the people that day. Six mothers made a commitment of their lives to the Lord Jesus.

The other biblical offensive weapon, prayer, is the Christian's unseen weapon. It can summon aid in an emergency or sustain strength and fortification for the long haul. We are commanded to "pray continually" (1 Thessalonians 5:17). And when one's prayers are in accord with other Christians' prayers, this is the ultimate weapon.

While all of this armor is G.I.—God's Issue—equipment, I

have found that different kinds of battles call for different strategies:

The powerful *name of Jesus* is mighty when deployed against the forces of darkness. The Lord Jesus Christ is the Son of God, sent from heaven to destroy the works of Satan on this planet and to redeem mankind from his hold over them. He is *the Lord*—the One with all authority in heaven and on earth. He is *Jesus*—the Savior and Deliverer from sin and death. He is *the Christ*—the Anointed One, the Messiah who came in fulfillment of prophecy.

These three parts of His name, written or spoken, have no great power in themselves, of course. But when invoked under the anointing of the Holy Spirit with the full significance of their meaning proclaimed to the powers of darkness, great authority and power are released from heaven.

On my visits to Arco Iris I would always invoke and plead the name of the Lord Jesus Christ before ever setting foot on the dump. The Lord taught me much about the power in this mighty name. His name stands for *Himself!* His very own presence. "His name shall be called Emmanuel—God with us." Even in Old Testament days, God's people knew that when they went into battle "in His name," He was going with them: "Through you we push back our enemies; through *your name* we trample our foes" (Psalm 44:5).

One day after returning from a joyful and spiritually fruitful visit to Arco Iris, I read the words of the Lord Jesus in John 17:26: "I have declared unto them thy name, and will declare it" (KJV). We all have much to learn about this "name above all names." As our knowledge and experience of it expand, so we shall be able to magnify, exalt and proclaim the character of our wonderful God. "O Lord, *our* Lord, how majestic is your name in all the earth!" (Psalm 8:9).

On the occasion of the witch's suspected curse at Arco Iris, I quickly reminded the forces of darkness that the *blood of the Lamb* had already been shed on the cross of Calvary to redeem me from my sins and to break Satan's power over me. As a child of God, I was literally off-limits to them. The devil and his companions had no right to interfere.

John, the beloved disciple, wrote:

> Then I heard a loud voice in heaven say: "Now have come the salvation and the power and the kingdom of our God, and the authority of his Christ. For the accuser of our brothers, who accuses them before our God day and night, has been hurled down. They overcame him by the blood of the Lamb and by the word of their testimony."
>
> Revelation 12:10–11

That curse at Arco Iris never landed! Obviously Satan and his guerilla band had to slink away impotently when confronted with the facts: my acceptance of the blood of Christ shed for me, and the reminder of Satan's defeat at the cross.

The *word of our testimony* is also vital in breaking down opposition to the Gospel from satanic forces. Some Christians are outspoken about denouncing "experiences" and insist that the only message worth proclaiming is the Word of God. Scripture itself disagrees, however, for the Word makes it clear that faith without works or action is dead (James 2:17). The devil knows that and so does the man or woman on the street who is waiting to see a practical demonstration of the great truths of God's Word, acted out in the daily lives of believers. Experience is true confirmation of belief.

When Christians quarrel and are bitter, resentful and envious of one another, the people about them will not be attracted to Christ. But when believers choose to give a "soft answer" in the midst of a heated dispute, or "turn the other cheek" to someone who has spoken unkindly, or pray for their enemies, the world will be convinced that there is something to Christianity, after all. We need both—bold declaration of the Word of God and convincing illustrations.

Getting these two essentials out of balance is another subtle trap of Satan. We may become so absorbed in the study of the Word, or in some issue such as spiritual warfare, that we find ourselves becoming proud, superior, domineering, impatient or withdrawn. It is also possible to spend so much time in the "doing" of Christian ministry that we lose touch with the Lord and His Word, and are no longer sensitive to His voice, thus setting ourselves up for an enemy ambush!

Praise that springs from the heart and spirit was one weapon I used constantly at Arco Iris. We began every meeting with the people on the dump with a prayer of thanksgiving, followed by songs of praise, knowing that the devil does not like to hear God's children praising their Father. He detests this because it is the one thing he wants for himself. That is why he rebelled against God in heaven and was cast out to earth, here to be an instrument later in testing the hearts of God's people. Our praise makes it clear that we wish God to receive glory—and, thus, routs the enemy.

In recent years, the Church has experienced new dimensions in praise and worship, and much blessing has resulted. As more and more believers desire to please God in their worship, they are seeking expressions outlined in the Scriptures. No longer concerned about inhibitions and traditions, they have either rejected old stereotyped forms of worship or infused them with new meaning. Some congregations now praise God with uplifted hands and dance as described in David's psalms, while others have studied the deeper symbolism of their liturgy and find God newly present in old forms. "Great is the Lord and most worthy of praise; his greatness no one can fathom. One generation will commend your works to another; they will tell of your mighty acts" (Psalm 145:3–4).

King David learned what we must learn, that it is the condition of the heart in worship that concerns the Lord. Unless we come in confession and repentance to our most awesome and holy God, the One who is pure love, righteousness and justice, we cannot possibly worship in spirit and in truth. To embark on a series of hymns, spiritual songs or choruses, or even a formal liturgy, without time to prepare one's heart first is to make worship a fraction of what it should be. And the devil is very much aware of our humanness. Even while on our knees, he will attempt to divert and confuse. Since we know the subtlety of his strategy, we can be ready for him.

When true worship is offered to God, something dynamic happens. The Lord comes and dwells in the midst of His people, and the devil must flee!

There comes a time in our warfare against the strongholds of the enemy when we know that the ruling power or principality has been cast down by the strong weapons God puts in our hands. A flood of blessing always accompanies the pulling down of an enemy stronghold.

We are "more than conquerors" when we walk in the victorious power of God's Spirit living within us. The torch of victory and the commission to go in and possess the land were handed to Jesus' disciples on the Day of Pentecost. Throughout the ages that torch has been handed on to succeeding generations, some of whom have barely kept the flame alight, while others have advanced the cause of Christ on a global scale.

One day I came home from Arco Iris and went down to the fruit plantation at Recanto to pick some fresh lemons for juice for the family. Two of the trees attracted my attention. One, which until that point had looked lush and full of life, was now brown and dry. The other, in sharp contrast, was covered with waxy foliage and plump, juicy fruit.

The odd thing was that when we had first arrived at Recanto, the second tree had appeared to be in a sorrier state than the first—merely a stick in the ground with a couple of bare twigs. It had apparently been stripped by soldier ants shortly after being planted. But now it was healthy.

As I examined the dead tree, I discovered that the tip had been snapped off at the top, about ten feet from the ground. For three years this tree had supplied us with scores of juicy lemons. Now its life was stunted, its process of growth impeded, its supply of fruit cut off. It was a sad sight.

A parable, with three distinct interpretations, came to mind as I studied the two trees:

1. An abandoned child may be taken into the care of loving Christian parents and grow up to be a healthy, useful member of society, while a normal, happy child may suddenly be destroyed socially, emotionally or mentally by the evil actions of others.

2. A church may be dying on the vine, but revived through the prayers of faithful members, while a church refusing to move on with the Lord can cut itself off from its source of fruitfulness.

3. A desperate sinner (like many on the rubbish dump) may turn to Christ and through the power of the Holy Spirit come into a radical relationship with the living God, while a dedicated believer (like myself) may become ensnared by the devil through pride, the temptation to disobey or other devious routes, opening the door to barrenness and death. I stood there a long time, considering these possibilities.

Today we have perhaps the last opportunity to seek our God for a great anointing and outpouring of His Holy Spirit so that we can fully appropriate all of the resources available to us in Christ Jesus to crush Satan under our feet (Romans 16:20).

The battle is on. We are commanded to take up arms, to watch and to pray. The enemy has marshaled his diabolical forces of darkness for his last great assault on the human race; in fact, it has already begun. Shall we sit any longer in dreamy contemplation, passive meditation or fearful prostration? Or shall we respond to the great challenge of the hour?

To those who pick up the torch and hold it high, the promise of the Lord is:

> "Arise, shine, for your light has come, and the glory of the Lord rises upon you. See, darkness covers the earth and thick darkness is over the peoples, but the Lord rises upon you and his glory appears over you."   Isaiah 60:1–2

The following prayer (adapted) by Victor Matthews is a model that we may use at the start of each day.

Prayer for Spiritual Warfare

Heavenly Father, I worship You and give You praise. I recognize that You are worthy to receive all glory and honor. I am thankful, heavenly Father, that You have loved me from past eternity and that You sent the Lord Jesus Christ into the world to die as my substitute, and that through Him You have completely forgiven me; You have adopted me into Your family; You have assumed all responsibility for me; You have given me eternal life; You have given me the perfect righteousness of the Lord Jesus Christ so that I am now justified. I am thankful that in Him You have made me complete, and that You have offered Yourself to me to be my daily help and strength.

I am thankful for the victory the Lord Jesus Christ won for me through His death and resurrection. Because of it, I am seated with the Lord in the heavenlies. I take my place with Him and recognize by faith that all wicked spirits and Satan himself are under my feet.

I am thankful for the armor You have provided. I put on the girdle of truth, the breastplate of righteousness, the sandals of peace and the helmet of salvation. I lift up the shield of faith against all the fiery darts of the enemy; and I take in my hand the sword of the Word of God. I choose to use Your Word against all the forces of evil in my life. I put on this armor and live and pray in complete dependence upon the Holy Spirit.

I claim all victory for my life today, rejecting all the insinuations, accusations and temptations of Satan. I choose, heavenly Father, to live in obedience and in fellowship with You. Open my eyes and show me the areas of my life that do not please You, and work in me to cleanse me from all that would give Satan a foothold against me.

I am thankful, heavenly Father, that the weapons of our warfare are not carnal but mighty through God to the pulling down of strongholds, to the casting down of imaginations and every high thing that exalts itself against the knowledge of God, and to bring every thought into obedience to the Lord Jesus Christ.

In my own life today, I tear down the strongholds of Satan and smash his plans that have been formed against me. I tear down the strongholds of Satan against my mind, and I surrender my mind to You, blessed Lord Jesus. I affirm, heavenly Father, that You have not given me the spirit of fear but of power and of love and of a sound mind.

I break and smash the strongholds of Satan formed against my emotions today. I give my will to you, Lord, and choose to make the right decisions of faith.

I smash the strongholds of Satan formed against my body today, and give my body to You, Lord, recognizing that I am Your temple.

Heavenly Father, I pray that now and through this day You will strengthen and enlighten me; show me the way Satan is hindering and tempting and lying and distorting the truth in my life. Enable me to be the kind of person that pleases You.

I abandon myself to You, heavenly Father. You have proven Your power by resurrecting Jesus Christ from the dead, and I claim this victory over all satanic forces in my life. I pray in the name of the Lord Jesus Christ with thanksgiving. Amen.

Even though I knew these principles, putting them into practice was not always easy. One more lesson that the Lord taught me about abandonment to Him involved serving my brothers, even though it made getting to my work at the dump more difficult. But then, I was used to the devil's tactics there. This was a new, niggling frustration. And obedience was the only way out of it.

11
The Kombi

"I will make peace
your governor
and righteousness
your ruler."
Isaiah 60:17

It did not appear to start as a lesson from the Lord. Adjacent to the rubbish dump was a car repair shop. In May 1983, our kombi was in need of a general overhaul, treatment for rust and a paint job. Having obtained a reasonable price estimate, I delivered the vehicle. In the meantime we would rent a car for the three-week scheduled work period.

At the end of the first week, I stopped by the shop to see how things were progressing. To my disappointment, I discovered that nothing had been done beyond removing all the windows. When I asked why, I was told that the worker who had been assigned the job had walked out. The owner said—halfheartedly, I felt—that he hoped to employ someone in his place.

A week later, on the first of June, I checked again on the work. Nothing had been done. The windowless kombi was still sitting there, covered in dust, and was beginning to look like an old wreck.

My heart sank. I knew I could not afford to rent a vehicle for any longer than the three weeks. It was clear that, even if someone started to work on the bus immediately, it would take a long time to finish the job. How could I get the milk to Arco Iris without transportation? How could I get Timothy to school in Atibaia every day?

These thoughts raced through my mind as I stared in dismay at the kombi. Then, noting an actual smirk on the face of one of the welders who seemed to be enjoying my discomfort, I lost even the thought of the Lord's peace. My blood began to boil.

I demanded to see the owner of the shop. When he appeared, I erupted in anger, embarrassing him thoroughly in front of his employees. I felt justified, but as soon as I finished my tirade, I realized I had violated a fundamental principle: a loving heart toward my neighbor. By forgetting that little frustrations make up a big part of the battle, I had grieved the Holy Spirit.

Later when I knelt before the Lord and confessed my sin, He poured in His healing balm and restored my soul. But along with the healing came the definite impression that I must apologize to the owner of the repair shop. This would be far from easy. Was the Lord trying to teach me something else through this frustrating experience?

The Lord showed me that I had to go back into that shop as His representative and allow Him to show His presence there. When the enemy is active—and sometimes we can actually feel the tension his presence brings—fear, doubt, distrust and despair abound, leading to outbursts of frustration and anger. If God's presence is manifest in the midst of the trouble by a servant of the Lord, however, the enemy has to flee.

God's presence is manifest by the Holy Spirit in love, joy, peace, patience, kindness, goodness, faithfulness, gentleness and self-control (see Galatians 5:22–23). I knew the Lord would have to do a miracle to take me into that shop with those qualities evident in my life, while the kombi sat there like a heap of old scrap!

He suggested that I begin by praying for every man in the place. Later, He showed me that the kombi would not be repaired until every man who worked there had had an opportunity to hear the Word of God. I was to go every day and read a passage from His Word that He would give me.

After much prayer and with more than a little trepidation, I set out one morning in a friend's borrowed car with my Bible. As I arrived at the repair shop, my first big test presented itself right away. The kombi had still not been touched! In spite of my past failure, in spite of the Lord's recent teaching and my own resolve not to get upset again, I felt the heat of anger rising in my flushed face.

Trembling with emotion, I stopped outside the door. An inner battle raged, fueled by the devil's attack on this chink in my armor. *Why are you here?* came the familiar small voice. *To check on the kombi or to present the Word of God to lost men?*

I knew why I had come, of course, but the anger and resentment had not dissipated. Still, I could not stand waiting outside the door forever. I had to go in and face those men.

I pushed open the door and stepped inside. The place was deserted, not a soul anywhere. I could not understand it. It was as if they knew what I had come for and scampered into hiding.

There was a wave of relief, but as I made my way home relief gave way to disappointment. Why had the Lord asked me so clearly to do something for Him that I was prevented from fulfilling? What was going on? Was this the enemy's work or the Lord's?

When I got home and continued to seek Him about it, He revealed to me that He indeed was in control. He had allowed that as an opportunity to test my true feelings about this assignment. Was I going into that shop to give the Word of God as His representative, or was I still preoccupied with the kombi?

Pierced through with conviction, I knew at once that I had not fully grasped the mind of God and was frustrating His purposes with my own thoughts, emotions and desires. Instead of carrying out His commands and instructions with singleness of heart, I was sidetracked by selfish interests.

Once again, I had to repent. This time, however, I was grateful that the Lord had spared me the embarrassment of making a fool of myself and that I had not dishonored Him again publicly.

That same afternoon I returned to the workshop with great peace in my heart and a spring in my step. I did not even glance at the kombi as I pushed the door open.

"Don't worry, fellows," I said with a grin on my face, "I'm not here to complain! I'm on far more important business. The Lord God has sent me to tell you that He's been looking for you. He wants you in His Kingdom."

One of the three men laid down his wrench and pushed back his cap with a greasy hand. The other two looked up, distracted momentarily from their work. No doubt it wasn't every day that someone stopped in to deliver a royal summons!

My grin widened now that I knew I had their attention.

"Yes, it's true. God wants to save you from your sins and give you His new life. The delay in the repair of the kombi is not your fault. He planned it this way!"

By now all three had moved a step closer. I told them that I would be coming every day to pass on the Lord's messages to them.

"Today He wants you to hear this," I said, flipping my Bible open to the book of Mark. " 'What good is it for a man to gain the whole world, yet forfeit his own soul?' Give that some thought today, and I'll see you tomorrow."

For six weeks the Lord supplied His words for those men and a borrowed vehicle to make the trip to the rubbish dump. Each time I entered the workshop, they listened attentively and with unusual respect. By the end of July I sensed that two of the men were near the Kingdom of God, and that the third had closed his heart to the Gospel. Considerable progress had been made on the kombi during this period, but it had not been reassembled or painted.

On a Monday morning I went in with the Scripture the Lord had given for that day. The foreman told me that the man who had been working on the kombi had left. Unless he could get a new mechanic, he explained apologetically, there would be a further delay since there were three other cars ahead of mine.

To my own great surprise I found myself saying, "I'm not worried. The most important thing is that you find the reality of Jesus Christ as your Savior and Lord. A motor vehicle is nothing compared to that!" We had a long chat about spiritual things, and for the first time he revealed some deep needs in his life.

The next day the Lord gave me a special, anointed word—John 3:27: "A man can receive only what is given him from heaven." Suddenly I knew that I would not receive the kombi until the Lord released it. Furthermore, He was not going to give it back unless I asked for it!

When our wills are aligned with God's will, He delights in answering our prayers. That is why He makes such startling promises as John 14:14: "You may ask me for anything in my name, and I will do it."

After receiving that special word from the Lord, I knew that I could ask for the kombi to be released and I would have it. My prayer reflected this new revelation, and I received it in faith.

On Tuesday and Wednesday I took in the Scriptures the Lord had given and each day noticed a marked change in the appearance of the kombi. Though I made no comment, inwardly I was praising the Lord. On Thursday I could not believe my eyes. There it stood, sparkling in its coat of fresh paint. By Saturday the car was fully assembled, ready for me to drive away and looking like a brand-new bus.

On that day the Lord had led me to 2 Corinthians 5:17: "Therefore, if anyone is in Christ, he is a new creation; the old has gone, the new has come!"

What a setup He was giving me to illustrate that verse! I pointed out to the men that there are only two alternatives for a worn-out automobile—the scrap heap or a face lift. But for a man, God offers something more—not just a paint job, but a brand-new nature, transformed from the inside out. God was ready to transform their lives, but they had to take the first step. My mission to them was complete. What happened now was between them and God.

Each time I think back on this incident, I am amazed all over again at the goodness of God in turning one of the most frustrating experiences of my life into one of the most thrilling. Abandonment to Him means staying alert to the devil's ragings every moment. But I saw as never before that, while surrendering all to Him would mean hard testing grounds, He would be faithful to train me to win.

12
Answers to Prayer

You have planted them,
and they have taken
root; they grow and
bear fruit.

Jeremiah 12:2

One day a young mother was waiting when I arrived at Arco Iris. She asked me if I would go with her to pray for an elderly widow named Dona Maria who had just returned from the hospital. The poor woman was recovering from an attack of a few days earlier during which she had been stabbed and robbed.

After serving all the children, I accompanied her, along with several other mothers, to see Dona Maria. As I entered the little hut, I was shocked to find the place littered with rubbish—piles of dirty paper, filthy bottles and smelly containers of all shapes and sizes. Flies buzzed everywhere, hundreds of them.

There were no windows in the hut, just cracks and gaping holes in the wooden-slatted walls. In the midst of all this disarray and chaos, the only furniture that could be seen were bare orange boxes, upended. These seemed to be full of ragged clothing.

On a simple bed covered with old cloths lay Dona Maria, obviously in great pain. After the robbery, she had been taken to the hospital and treated, then discharged—prematurely, I concluded from her appearance.

In all of my experience with the poor, I had never seen anyone so destitute or in such great need. I felt absolutely helpless. Nevertheless, I called on the Lord to reveal Himself to Dona Maria, touch her life with His presence and supply her needs. And He answered within an hour or so, arranging for her to be returned to the Santa Casa Hospital at Atibaia, where she stayed until she made a full recovery.

The Lord spoke loudly to me through that experience. If I was shocked at the physical and material privation of Dona Maria, how would I feel if I could see the utter spiritual destitution of a soul without God? *As great as is the physical need of the poor,* the Lord seemed to be saying, *the spiritual need of the lost is far greater. What is the long-term benefit of a sack of rice to a starving man if he continues to live in sin and self-gratification, and ends up in a Christless eternity?*

Suddenly the milk and candy I had been bringing to the children living on the dump seemed woefully inadequate. These people needed much more. They needed food, yes. But they needed meat and vegetables and fruit. And their spiritual hunger could not be satisfied through flannelgraph lessons forever. Besides, what would happen to them if I got sick or was called away? The thought was sobering.

For months now, Heather and I had encouraged our prayer partners to join us in praying that the Lord would touch one of the families to open up their home for prayer meetings and Bible studies in order to ground the new converts in the principles of the Christian life. This became a critical concern for us as we struggled to keep up with the growing needs.

Living on the rubbish dump was an alcoholic mother named Dona Elsa. She appeared frequently at the Sunday afternoon meetings looking miserable and dejected. Although her children had left home and she was living alone, she had made it a habit to ask for milk and anything else we might be distributing.

One Sunday Dona Elsa turned up in a terrible state. She was at the point of desperation, not knowing how to free herself from the terrible craving for alcohol. It so happened that our son Andrew, who had completed two years of service with Operation Mobilization, was spending a few days with us to introduce his friend Gaynor, who was later to become his life partner. Andrew and Gaynor were with me on the dump, praying for the worshipers as I led the service.

That afternoon, Dona Elsa hung on every word of the message, and to my surprise, at the conclusion, surrendered her life to Jesus Christ. One had only to look into her eyes to know the sincerity of her conversion.

Gaynor then took Dona Elsa aside and led her through a prayer of deliverance from her addiction to drink. After this prayer Dona Elsa was radiant! Truly a new person in Christ Jesus!

Dona Elsa's daughter, who was already a believer, lived and worked in Sao Paulo. When next she visited her mother and discovered the remarkable change in her, she was overjoyed at God's miracle of grace. In praying together, they felt impressed to build a small prayer chamber on the rubbish dump, next to Dona Elsa's shack.

With the help of believers from her daughter's church in Sao Paulo, the little hut was constructed. All this was kept a closely guarded secret from me, as the site of the building was on the opposite side of the dump to where we held the services.

When the construction was completed, they announced at the end of the next open-air Sunday meeting that they had a surprise for me.

"Pastor, come and see what we have built!" Dona Elsa said with shining eyes. I went hesitantly, not having the least idea what she was going to show me. She pointed to a wooden shed, which looked just like one of the better-class homes on the dump. The words *Casa de Oracao* were painted in shaky lettering above the door: "House of Prayer."

A great joy flooded my heart as I entered. The inside was freshly painted white and was quite bare except for a few hand-made wooden benches. But this was indeed a church—a true sanctuary!

I could hardly believe my eyes. Now we had a real church made available to us. Our prayers had indeed been answered.

Shortly thereafter a letter from our daughter Susan in England brought a somber note into our lives.

"Dear Mum and Dad, So sorry to be the bearer of bad news, but thought you ought to know that Grandma is ill. She says I shouldn't bother you, since you were only here for a visit a few months ago, but of course you have to know. . . ."

My mother's illness was only part of our dilemma. Having legally adopted little John, Sara and Daniel according to Brazilian law, we had learned through the British consulate that to have their adoptions recognized at home in England, we must establish permanent residency there and readopt them in the British courts.

How could we return to England both to care for my mother and obtain the adoption papers for our children without abandoning the work at Arco Iris? The answer, of course, lay in prayer, in seeking God's will, with the aid of our many prayer partners who had followed all these developments through weekly prayer letters.

Several Brazilian Christian workers had helped with the ministry at the dump at various times, and we were deeply grateful to God for them. None, however, had the time or financial backing to take the work over.

As we concentrated our prayers on this issue, we saw God do a beautiful thing right under our noses! The questions that were causing us the most concern in finding God's choice for the supervision of the work were: a) the need for a person who had a genuine affinity for the rubbish dump folk; b) the need for a real commitment, especially in view of the atrocious conditions on the dump; 3) the need for a person with great sensitivity and understanding of children and their mothers.

One person amply fulfilled every requirement. She herself lived on the dump. Her heart was on fire for the Lord, and she had a burden to show Christ's love to those around her. And, frankly, the work required the sensitivity of a woman to deal with some of the recent problems that were arising. Dona Elsa!

As we commenced the weekday prayer meetings and Bible studies in the little church, Dona Elsa shared with me her deep gratitude to God for what He had done in her life. On her own initiative, she had already started a Sunday school and a class to teach the children how to read. Her conversion was genuine, and she was totally committed to serving the Lord who had delivered her.

Dona Elsa's work with the children was soon backed by the local authorities in Atibaia, who supplied her with educational materials and encouraged her in every way possible. The House of Prayer was a school by day and a church by night. It was obvious that she was handpicked by the Lord to care for His flock in this difficult place!

She moved into the leadership role just as Heather and I felt the Lord moving us out. We were ready to face the next mission He had for us.

In Brazil there lives an unusual bird called the toucan. His name derives from his cry as he glides from branch to branch in the Amazon forests: "Two can! Two can!" When Heather and I heard that call, we were reminded that "*two can* live better than one can. *Two can* accomplish more than one can. *Two can* serve God better than one can!"

The family unit has always been a prime target of Satan, and over the past decade he seems to have stepped up his offensive. He knows that the failure of a marriage is an easy way to introduce bitterness, despair and resentment against God, which in turn can lead to moral laxity and every kind of sin and abuse, spiraling downward to utter destruction.

Christian marriages are especially subject to attack. From our experience the more closely we try to walk with the Lord, the fiercer the onslaughts against us. Does this mean we should cease walking with the Lord and trying to live in His will? Of course not! For as we learn to apply the principles of spiritual warfare in this most intimate relationship of life, we thwart the enemy's plan to destroy our marriage.

If you had been our neighbor in Brazil, you might have caught Heather and me in some tense moments. We found that, especially before visits to Arco Iris or critical preaching engagements, the enemy would attack at the point of our greatest vulnerability. It still happens occasionally, usually just before the Lord is going to break through to us in a dramatic way.

Two hearts that have been united by God are held together by supernatural bonds, supernatural love and power. If we forget that fact and resort to natural means to resolve problems in our lives, we give entrance to the enemy whose express purpose is in destroying all that we have built together.

Heather and I are learning to spot the signs of this activity and to stand against it, but we are sometimes slow to apply all the principles the Lord has been teaching us over the past twelve years. We shudder at the responsibility placed on our shoulders when the Lord called us into His service with Luke 12:48: "From everyone who has been given much, much will be demanded; and from the one who has been entrusted with much, much more will be asked."

Many times through Heather's ministry God has humbled me

or prevented my taking a wrong turn. She is often able to see things I cannot see. Pride and self-determination also act as a barrier to the revelation of God's will and purpose in our lives, but a partner can tactfully point these out if the heart is open to correction. If not, there is always prayer!

Jesus said, "What God has joined together, let man not separate" (Mark 10:9). If any Christian man or woman is under fire from the enemy with thoughts or temptations about giving up on marriage, let him or her consider those words carefully.

It would soon be time to leave Brazil. For one of my last Sunday afternoon services, I presented to the Christians at the dump a beautiful banner, embroidered by a Sunday school group in England: "We are all one in Christ Jesus." My message followed this theme, fired by my new understanding of our unity in Him.

With fresh fervor, I told the congregation of poor folk that when a sinner repents of his sin and turns to Jesus for salvation, he becomes a new creation, a brand-new person, a member of God's family.

"You become my brother or my sister," I said, looking into the eager faces, "for we are in the same family. I become your *brother*. In fact, you are more closely related to me than my own relatives who don't know Jesus."

I could tell that this new thought was having an effect and, when the appeal was made, a number of mothers and children came forward for prayer and counsel. One of these was a little girl of about eight. I had noticed her upturned, dark-skinned face and solemn eyes the whole time I had been speaking. She had obviously sensed the Lord's presence in our midst and heard His voice calling her to be a member of His family.

Now she stood with bowed head as I invited those who had

come forward to pray with me a prayer of commitment: "Lord Jesus, thank You for loving me so much that You died for me on the cross. I confess I have sinned and gone my own way. But now I turn to You. Be my Savior, my Lord and my King. Come and live within me. Fill me and equip me with your Holy Spirit so that I can be a light for You in this world of darkness. Thank You, Jesus. Amen."

As one after another made a commitment to the Lord, we sensed an awesome wonder filling our hearts. The miracle of new birth was taking place before our eyes. The little girl's face was aglow with radiant joy. Her shoulders were straighter, her head high and she looked at me out of eyes shining with a profound peace and joyous anticipation of a bright future. It seemed as if I could envision the beautiful young woman she would become, serenely rising above the dire circumstances of her birth and taking the place that had been ordained for her before the foundations of the earth.

Then she jolted me out of my reverie. "Thank you, my brother," she said softly.

Yes, this was now my little sister in Christ. And nothing in our backgrounds—neither race nor culture, neither class, literacy nor circumstances of birth—could alter that relationship through all eternity. We were family.

I looked at Dona Elsa, who would be giving herself to the ministry and at all the others who had made professions of faith during the time of our ministry at the dump. It seemed to me that I was leaving the situation in good hands. All the battles had not yet been won, but those souls in the Kingdom of God could more than hold their own against the powers of darkness there. I committed them to the One who prayed, "My prayer is not that you take them out of the world but that you protect them from the evil one" (John 17:15).

The people at Arco Iris and I were not so different after all. But for the grace of God I could be one of them, scrabbling in the dust and rubbish for a day's living, dependent upon the God of the abandoned who "provides food for those who fear him" (Psalm 111:5). But I also knew that each believer before me was a new creation in Christ Jesus. What a thrill it had been to bring God's good news to them!

When God had flung down the gauntlet to me many years before, and I had responded in an impassioned pledge to follow Him no matter what, even if it meant being a *dustman,* a refuse collector, I could not have known where it would lead me. It had led to life more abundant than I could have dreamed. And it had led to death . . . and beyond!

And now as we said goodbye to our friends at Arco Iris, I was sure the last chapter of that pledge had not been written. There would be other lessons, more miles to travel in my journey toward abandonment in Him.

I could not wait to begin!

Great are the works of the Lord;
   they are pondered by all who
   delight in them. . . .
He has caused his wonders to be
   remembered; the Lord is
   gracious and compassionate. . . .
The fear of the Lord is the beginning
   of wisdom; all who follow his
   precepts have good understanding.
   To him belongs eternal praise.
                              Psalm 111:2, 4, 10

Afterword

Ray and Heather Saunders are currently residing in Warminster, England, where Ray has a Bible teaching and preaching ministry among Christians of all denominations. Here are updates on their six children:

Susan Joy (32) and her husband, Mick Taylor, have three children, Paul, Johnny and Ruth. Sue continues to be her mother's prayer partner. "We don't ever feel parted from Sue."

Andrew (30) and Gaynor have five children, Shalomir, Joshua, and recently adopted infant twins, Rachel and Rebekah, and two-year-old David. Called to full-time mission service, Andrew ministers currently with the Good Shepherd Trust, serving the abandoned children of Brazil.

Timothy (19) was graduated from high school with honors in 1989. Now he is at the University of Leeds in northern England preparing for a career in international law, possibly to expedite the adoption of abandoned children.

John (10) is loving, sensitive, generous, considerate of others. He is also musically gifted, both vocally and instrumentally.

Sara (10) is Heather's "right hand," an answer to prayer when Susan left home to marry. She is artistic, responsible and a good student.

Daniel (9) is athletic, despite his "handicap." He is more often on his head than on his feet! Playful and fun-loving, he is a delight to have around.

The greatest lesson of all for Heather and Ray is not the realization that one must die to self, but that it is a daily and a moment-by-moment surrender of one's will to God. Though He may give a vision of His purpose for a life, the fulfillment of that vision may be a lengthy process—indeed, even a lifelong process.

Still, those who are fully Christian are not "resigned" to the will of God, or acquiescent in it, or just conformed by it; they are abandoned to it!

For details of the Good Shepherd Trust, serving homeless children in Brazil, write to:

> The Secretary
> Good Shepherd Trust
> Twineham Place Farm, Twineham
> Haywards Heath
> Sussex RH17 5NP
> England